Federica
Thank you,

The Rest of It

with love
Maureen

MAUREEN MULLALLY-CLARKE

For my children – Hugh, Maureen, Tom,
Alice, Katie, Nora and Mary Rose.

And my grandchildren – John, Katie, Fiona, James,
Tom, Alex, Siobhán, Will, Róisín, Tara,
Georgia, Ciarán, Rosie and my great-grandson Arlo William

And in loving memory of Kate Finnigan, Oonagh
and John Keefe, Tommy and Maureen McAleer,
Jimmy and Michael McAleer, John Mullally,
Neil Clarke and Anne Toal.

Many thanks to Sebastian at Battersea Place for the cover photo.

ISBN: 978-1-913637-37-8

Editor: Shaun Russell & Keren Williams

Printed and bound in the UK by
4edge, 22 Eldon Way, Hockley, Essex, SS5 4AD

Published by
Jelly Bean Books
Mackintosh House
136 Newport Road, Cardiff, CF24 1DJ, Wales, UK
www.candyjarbooks.co.uk

- CHAPTER ONE -
A LATE STARTER

The phone call cost tuppence in 1951. It was from one of those red telephone boxes somewhere along the Strand between King's College and Charing Cross Station. I made the call with the thought that this was the most important day of my life so far. Little did I realise just how important it was actually going to be.

When my mother answered the call I told her my exciting news. I had been accepted by the Dean of the law faculty at King's to study for my LL.B, my law degree, starting the following October. As I was already twenty-one years old, there had been some doubt whether I would be considered a suitable candidate for admission, but Professor Graveson told me that he thought I would be a steadying influence on the other six younger girls in my year – the remaining thirty-three students being young men of course, in those days.

When she had joined in my excitement Mummy said, 'Hurry home, your father has someone coming for an interview, and I want you to give me a hand with the tea.'

Poor Daddy had been suffering dreadfully from sciatica. As a GP he had needed a locum to take care of his patients; an elderly Irish practitioner had been living with us for several months, but he had decided to return to his family in Ireland the following January, when the contract with my father came to an end.

'Doctie', as my irrepressible sister Oonagh christened him for family use, had become very fond of my youngest brother, then not quite a year old. He told my parents that he had a grandchild of the same age, but had never seen him. Apparently, his daughter had married someone of whom he disapproved. Like many an Irish parent in the same circumstances, my paternal grandfather for instance, his response had been to refuse her his forgiveness, or even have any desire to meet his grandchild.

But daily contact with little Michael had changed his mind. He went to the best toy shops to match the toys that Mikey liked to play with, and was flying back to Dublin with a suitcase packed full of them, intending to surprise his daughter by letting bygones be bygones so far as the unsuitable marriage was concerned.

My abiding memory of Doctie is of him pursuing my mother around the kitchen table, syringe at the ready in his hand. Mummy had been prescribed injections for some malady and was terrified of the needles, but Doctie was a determined little man and he won the battles.

So the person coming for an interview was to be a replacement for Doctie. John Mullally was eleven years older than me. Qualified in 1945, he had gone straight into the RNVR as a ship's surgeon on naval supply vessels operating between Hong Kong, Singapore and Hiroshima, still a wasted desert resulting from the atomic bomb explosion there.

Having finished his term of service with the Royal Navy, John had continued his seafaring by enlisting with the Union Castle line – travelling between the UK and South Africa for several years providing medical care for the passengers on their luxury liners.

When he turned thirty he decided to 'swallow the anchor', as they say, and settle down as a general practitioner. His preferred option would have been to go home to Tipperary but, as he explained, to find a practice in Ireland at the time you had to be either the son of a doctor or related to a bishop.

Possessing neither of these advantages, the choice was between the United States and England. His friends who could afford the costs of getting there and re-qualifying chose America, but England was the only real possibility for him.

Initially, he worked as an assistant in a practice in Worksop, a coal mining area. There being no chance of getting a partnership there, he was looking around for an opportunity elsewhere in the country, preferably near London where he already had several Irish friends. There were no such posts available in the weeks coming up to Christmas, so he had decided to take the one and only locum he ever did, which would give him a chance to look around. And that's how we met that December afternoon.

Later he always told me that he made up his mind to marry me then and there. But as far as I was concerned he was definitely one of the grown-ups, tall, chunky and good-looking, but much more of my parents' generation than mine.

He moved in with us to take over from Doctie on

10th January 1952. To be frank, he made anything but a good start as far as I was concerned. My parents and I had been invited to a party that night to which a young poet, whose name I have now forgotten, had also been invited. I was keen to meet him, but I had a bit of a cold.

Daddy thought it was too wintry for me to be going out. Very unfairly, he put the responsibility on John, who had only just arrived. 'If she were your daughter,' he asked him, 'would you let her go out with a cold on a night like this?'

John was on a hiding to nothing and had no alternative but to express agreement with my father's concerns, as Daddy had anticipated. So no party for me.

Furious, I marched off to my bedroom and sulked until my parents had left. Oonagh came up shortly afterwards to say, 'The locum wondered if you would like him to make you a cup of tea.'

I accepted the tea but with very bad grace and no intention of forgiving him.

The phone had been plugged in beside John's bed in the spare room because he would have been responsible for taking any night calls from Daddy's practice. There was a call during the night, but it was not made by a patient, it was from a police officer. For some reason we never understood, the only phone number they had for Doctie was ours. The Aer Lingus plane carrying him home to Dublin had crashed in the Welsh mountains. The plane was a small one, a Dakota, and there were only twelve passengers, plus three crew members. The weather had been shocking, gale force winds, driving rain and terrible visibility. There were no survivors.

John had to wake my sleeping parents and ask for Doctie's home telephone number in Ireland to give to the police officer on the other end of the line.

We were all really shocked and upset about poor Doctie. Knowing that his reunion with his daughter was to be a surprise, my mother wrote to express our sympathy for the family's tragic loss. She explained what his plan had been and how he had been bringing a suitcase full of toys for the grandchild he had never seen.

Meanwhile, John was settling into our family circle and becoming very popular with Daddy's patients in his absence.

At the time, my boyfriend was Peter, the son of an army colleague of Daddy's who happened to live around the corner from us. Peter and I met when we were about thirteen years old and began to go out together when we were seventeen. At eighteen he had to do his two years of military service, as all young men were compelled to do at the time, but he enjoyed it so much that he took a permanent commission in the Army.

We wrote to one another when he was away on overseas duty and continued to 'date', as it was called, whenever he was on leave. It was a very innocent relationship, as dating tended to be in those days. Daddy was not completely happy about the idea that I might end up married to an Army officer, but Peter was a Catholic, so got top marks for that.

As a matter of fact, Daddy was very strict when it came to boyfriends. If they did not happen to be Catholic they would very quickly be shown the door.

Oonagh was a medical student by that time and, on one occasion, brought a fellow student called Reg home to tea. Reg was a completely inoffensive young man, well-mannered and public school educated.

None of this commended him to my father. The minute Daddy's none-too-subtle inquisition had elicited from the poor boy that he was in fact an Anglican, Daddy's fierce bushy eyebrows drew together, a sure sign that he was cross with one of us.

As soon as the front door had closed on Reg, Oonagh was instructed never to bring him to our home again.

But Oonagh was by no means a pushover, even for our father. I think the fact that she was already in love with her future husband, also called John, had a lot more to do with her compliance with Daddy's strictures than any desire to fall in with them, which I would inevitably have done.

Shortly after John took up residence with us, Peter called to take me to the cinema. John kindly helped him on with his coat as we left. Walking on our way to the village, Peter said, 'That locum has his eye on you.'

'Don't be so ridiculous,' I said. 'He's far too old for me.' And that is exactly what I thought.

Then, one day when his three weeks were nearly over, John came into the sitting room where Oonagh and I were reading and said, 'Any of you lads like to come to the cinema?'

Oonagh told me afterwards that she didn't feel this general invitation was intended for her, so kindly made some excuse. This time the trip to the village was in

John's car, not on foot.

I think I remember that the film was called *Monsieur Verdoux.* Rather to my surprise I found that John was holding my hand during the performance. I did find myself wondering if he had absent-mindedly mistaken me for someone else. On the journey back he didn't mention it to me and I didn't mention it to him.

Very shortly after that, John left to pursue his ambition to find a job near London. It was hard to find openings for GPs at the time, so in the end he took another post as assistant in a practice in Woolwich where his friend Anne Toal was already working.

He did, however, keep coming back to visit us, asking for Daddy's advice about various possible job opportunities. Daddy was very pleased about this, remarking to my mother that it was a great compliment that John thought so much of his advice.

'Tommy,' my mother said. 'He's not coming back just to see you.'

In March, John invited me to the annual St Patrick's Day ball at Grosvenor House Hotel in London. He wanted me to meet his friends. I was very excited about this, but I was in for a bit of a shock. When I had been to Army balls with Peter, or been invited to dances by other young men, my partners would invariably spend all the time looking after me, as was the English habit.

As soon as we hit the ballroom, and he had introduced me to the dozen or so friends who were in our party, John shot off to shake hands with – it seemed to me – almost every other guest present.

Leaving me with this crowd of strangers, he would

rush back at intervals to say something like, 'You're the best-looking girl in the room,' and then take off again, apparently to make sure he was right.

That was the first time I met Anne and her husband Frank, who was a close friend of John's, and had invited him to be best man at their wedding a few months earlier. Anne, as always, was kindness itself to me from that first meeting onwards. Much later, she told me that she had assumed I had an older sister that John was interested in.

The friends were longing to know why John had brought me to the ball. In those days, every man in a party would invite every girl to dance. One man confided in me when he was carrying out this duty that all John's friends were hoping he would marry Allie, Anne's sister.

For these and other reasons, the ball was not the most enjoyable occasion for me.

But after that John kept inviting me out and I was soon falling in love with him, poor Peter forgotten. Daddy was not best pleased with this development and would often warn me seriously not to set my heart on a 'typical Irish bachelor'.

Matters were not assisted when John took me to a popular French film called *La Ronde,* describing ten amorous encounters spread across the social spectrum, from a prostitute to a nobleman, each scene involving a character from the previous episode. Daddy was less than amused when on the following Sunday a screaming headline in his favourite newspaper read, 'Would you let your daughter see this film?'

Basically, Daddy was never convinced that there

would be any future in my relationship with John, and was trying to protect me from the heartbreak he was sure would be the outcome.

I went on hoping. Not that John gave me any encouragement to hope. Invariably, when he brought me back home after some outing, he would say, 'I'll give you a ring.' Never once did he suggest a date for the following week, or indeed any time in the future. However, he did seem very fond of me when we were together and we saw one another frequently.

For me, his lovely Tipperary accent was one of the most attractive things about him. Oonagh was characteristically merciless about it – telling me, 'It's "hall-*ooo*" again!' if she happened to be the one who picked up his phone call.

On my twenty-second birthday in July he gave me a very nice handbag with a card depicting a parrot. The printed inscription read: 'From one of them birds of damn few words.' He hadn't even signed it!

He knew I was starting at King's in the October. *Surely*, I thought, *he'll ask me to marry him before then and I can cancel the degree course.* When that did not happen I resigned myself to acceptance that Daddy, as usual, was right. John was destined to be a typical Irish bachelor.

- CHAPTER TWO -
WHY THE LATE START?

The other students in my year at King's were all school leavers, eighteen years old. I was the only twenty-two-year-old. Perhaps this deserves some explanation. At the end of my school career my A-level results were good enough to have secured a university place for me. Unfortunately, senior school had not been a very happy experience. I had been the subject of mild bullying until I was about fifteen, having completely failed to become the popular girl of my childhood dreams. My tormentors were the cleverest girls and were all off to various establishments of further education. It seemed to me at that point that I did not want to do the same. I would be meeting girls there who would be just as likely to bully me.

To the considerable and undisguised disappointment of my parents, I adamantly refused to consider applying to university. Daddy had always been insistent on Oonagh and me acquiring what he called 'a meal ticket', some qualification which would entitle us to earn ourselves a living.

In the absence of my ambition for higher education, he decided that he would spend the money instead on sending me to a secretarial college. At that time the two most highly regarded establishments in London were

St James's or Mrs Hoster's. Daddy chose St James's.

The college was situated just behind Buckingham Palace, which meant that we girls – there were no men – had an unrivalled bird's eye view of all the royal garden parties if we climbed to the top floor, which we invariably did when one was taking place. We learned Pitman's shorthand, touch typing and basic accountancy skills and we all qualified with good shorthand and typing skills, although so far as I was concerned proficiency in accountancy was never going to be achievable – too much maths involved.

I enjoyed my time at St James's and made some good friends there. Once qualified, we had no trouble finding jobs; the reputation of the college opened many doors. My first employment was as secretary to Miss Edwards who was the head of the education department in Macmillan, the publishing company, at that time situated only a short walk from Charing Cross Station. As I had always loved books, it was perfect for me.

Macmillan was very much a family firm. In my time it was headed by Mr Daniel. Mr Harold was also employed there, but was rather disapproved of by the family because he was more interested in politics than the really important business of publishing. The view seemed to be that he was a bit of a lightweight for this reason, even though he did end up as prime minister.

I remember him as a thoroughly charming gentleman of the old school. There was a canteen serving lunches in the basement of the building, and he appeared there one day when I was having a meal with my friends, apparently anxious to see how it all worked. The routine had to be explained to him, as it must have been the first time he had visited.

His wife, Lady Dorothy, appeared in the office periodically. She always looked a bit dishevelled to me, although her manner was very grand, the result no doubt of her aristocratic parentage – her father was the Duke of Devonshire. Years later, I heard that she had been romantically involved with Bob Boothby at the time. I cannot imagine a greater contrast from lovely Mr Harold.

In my day at Macmillan I now realise that the affair with Boothby was an open secret, but at that time the Establishment managed to keep anything of this sort out of the press. Harold remained devoted to his wife and refused her the divorce she wanted, even though her relationship with Boothby lasted for decades.

It was while I was at Macmillan that my parents told us that we were to have a new brother or sister. I was twenty, Oonagh eighteen, and Jimmy thirteen. Mummy would have been in her early forties. At that time it was fairly unusual for a woman of that age to have a baby, even though it is a commonplace event nowadays.

It seems incredible that – even though my father was a doctor and my mother had already given birth to three children – neither of them could understand the symptoms my mother had. Daddy made an appointment with the best gynaecologist in Harley Street. Mummy was subjected to an X-ray in the days when X-rays were ridiculously strong, and it was discovered that she was expecting Michael. Sadly, that was very early on in the pregnancy and Mike was born with a deformity of the spine, which I believe was directly attributable to that X-ray.

When they broke the news to us Daddy seemed to think that Oonagh and I would be disapproving. On the contrary we were both thrilled about it. Jimmy, already at boarding school, did not receive it quite so enthusiastically, and when Mike was born he wrote home, 'Maybe you'll think about me sometimes.'

On arrival the baby was rather underweight and very reluctant to feed. Initially, Mummy actually fed him with the filler intended for a fountain pen, rather than a bottle with a teat which would have been too large for him to cope with. But he had not one but three devoted mothers. Oonagh and I were more than keen to be able to help with him. Gradually he made progress as the subject of so much loving care.

Miss Edwards, a very formal lady who never invited me to call her by her Christian name even though we shared a room, unexpectedly presented me with a cuddly toy for Mike, which in fact became his favourite plaything.

I think she was quite disappointed when I told her that I was giving my notice as I had been told of a job opportunity which I simply couldn't resist. She had trained me to be a good proofreader, which was an important aspect of my job, and now she would have to start all over again with some novice. But she wished me well and we parted without any ill-feeling.

Daddy's best friend at medical school in Glasgow had become Medical Director for Canadian Pacific shipping. He wondered if I would like to have a summer covering for the leave of seagoing stenographers who worked in the pursers' offices of the three huge liners, one of which left Liverpool for Canada in weekly rotation. It says a lot about the progress I had made in self-confidence that I was prepared to take this on.

So, in July of that year, I set out on my first voyage, even though it meant that my twenty-first birthday would be spent onboard.

The Empress of France, the Empress of Canada and the Empress of Scotland left Liverpool in a weekly schedule; the voyages took three weeks to complete, and included a half day in Quebec followed by a trip up the St Lawrence river to Montreal, where the ships, which were grain carriers as well as passenger liners, spent two and a half days to allow for the unloading and loading of cargo.

Before I could take up this employment it was necessary for me to have my Seaman's Record Book, a sort of identity card in which each voyage would be recorded, together with comments on my 'ability' and 'general conduct'. I invariably got 'very good' for both, but I think the behaviour of a 'seaman' would have had to be pretty deplorable to earn anything less.

Naturally, I was nervous when I joined my first ship. Two stenographers worked in each Purser's Office, together with three young men who were assistant pursers. I was given a kind welcome by my new shipmates who were rather surprised by my youth. Apparently you had to be twenty-five to get a permanent appointment. When I got to know my friends better they told me that the 'Old Man', as they called the ship's captain, had lined them up before my arrival to tell them that I was the daughter of friend of their Medical Director, 'And if any of you lay a finger on her, you'll have me to answer to!'

I never had anything but respect from those young men. They soon realised how naive I really was and were determined to look after me, which they did kindly and well. My work was not demanding, just typing incredibly long manifests which set out all the details of the passengers, many of whom were emigrating to Canada. The worst part was that there were about six copies of these documents with carbon paper sheets between each page. If you mistyped, you had to put little correction papers under each carbon to delete the mistake, then remove the correction slips and retype. That could be immensely tedious but it sure made for accurate typing.

The other common hazard was that, in rough seas, the typewriter would jump the wooden 'fiddles' surrounding it for safety, drop to the floor and pursue me round the office. I very soon learned how to dodge a rogue machine without getting my ankles hacked.

One part of the pursers' job was to organise entertainment on the ships. When I saw 'horse racing' on the daily programme I begged to be allowed to visit the horses, as I assumed they would be below decks. No wonder they laughed.

Outside office hours life was amazing. We ate with the passengers – not the first-class ones of course, but I had never in my life seen anything like the menus, remember that food rationing was still strict back home. We would have five-course dinners – no wonder

I remained a bit plump!

My friends arranged a little party for my twenty-first, and the Captain sent down a bottle of sherry. I had no idea he knew of my existence.

When we arrived in Quebec we were all going to go ashore for dinner and the others were arranging a kitty for the evening. I asked what everyone was putting in and was told, 'Everyone on this ship is on some kind of con except you and the Old Man – and we're not even sure about him.'

So my contribution was refused. We went ashore in the afternoon and I simply couldn't believe the contents of the shop windows. Again, clothes rationing was still in force in the UK. I quickly discovered that most of the shopkeepers refused to speak English, although they were all fluent in the language, because the inhabitants of the province were defiantly sure they were French, and wanted English speakers to know it. For once I was useful to my shipmates because I had spent three months in a French family after leaving school.

That evening, we dined on spare ribs, delicious strips of pork on the bone cooked in a fantastic sauce and eaten with your hands. I soon realised why we had all been issued with massive bibs on taking our seats at the table.

The following day we sailed up the St Lawrence to Montreal, a voyage of the most breathtaking scenery whatever the time of year, but especially so in the autumn (or fall as I learned to call it) and winter. Montreal was even more amazing than Quebec, with its skyscraper buildings and even more fantastic shops.

With my earnings I bought a couple of dresses without coupons, a huge cuddly teddy for Mike and some packets of Betty Crocker cake mixes for Mummy.

In all I made five trips to Canada on the various Empresses. The total time I spent on shore there amounted to just under two weeks. There was plenty of fun to be had on the ships with my new friends, but I also had a good deal of time for reflection. Walking around the deck or just watching the sea or the St Lawrence flow past me, I began to think seriously about the future. I had already had two of the most wonderful jobs which secretarial skills could bring me. What did I want to do next? I was now attracted by the idea I had so strenuously resisted earlier. I would like to go to university, but how could I tell poor Daddy who had expended so much money on St James's?

When I came home for the last time, in about October, my parents already had an interview lined up for me with a local solicitor friend, Joyce Pinney. Dutifully, I walked to the village for my interview and was duly offered the post.

Walking home I thought, *I don't want to be Joyce Pinney's secretary, I want to be Joyce Pinney.* That evening, I told my parents that I wanted to study law. It must have been a bit of a shock, there I was with my good 'meal ticket', financially no longer a burden, but actually able to contribute to the household budget. And Daddy was not at all well off and suffering terrible sciatic pain. He said nothing about these matters but accepted my change of heart with his usual loving generosity. If that was really what I wanted, he would do everything in his power to support me. Oonagh was already studying medicine in London and living at home, if I could get into a London college I would be able to live at home too, so it was decided that I would apply to King's. As we already know, on the day that my application succeeded I met my future husband.

- CHAPTER THREE - KING'S

Apparently, Daddy had been right all along. John had indeed turned out to be a 'typical Irish bachelor'. To be fair, he had never given me the slightest encouragement to think otherwise: the unsigned parrot birthday card, the only Irish postcard he ever sent me signed baldly 'John', and always ending an evening with, 'I'll give you a ring', although neither of us in any doubt that he did not mean the kind you put on your finger.

I was in love with him, but he hadn't given a lot of evidence that he was in love with me. Clearly matrimony was the last thing on his mind, or he would have asked me to talk about it before my first university term began in October. I would happily have discarded my degree course if he had asked me to marry him. But there it was: he didn't.

Luckily I had acquired a lot of resilience and a certain amount of common sense since leaving school as a timid teenager, completely lacking in any self-confidence. St James's, Macmillan and Canadian Pacific had seen to that.

I turned up for my first law lecture determined to make a success of my studies. Not quite the start I was planning for, however. Whether the train was late or the bus was caught in traffic, I arrived at the magnificent lecture hall ten minutes after the lecture had begun. The lectern was sited immediately to the left of the entrance door.

I entered to find Professor Sir David Hughes Parry, distinguished author of *The Sanctity of Contract in English Law* no less, well into his dissertation on the leading case of *Donoghue v Stevenson,* something about someone finding a decomposed snail in her bottle of ginger beer and the identity of the person legally responsible for this horrible experience under the law of contract. He turned and regarded me with distaste, pausing reluctantly in response to my interruption.

Facing me were the serried ranks of my fellow students, row upon row of them climbing to the ceiling at the back of the room. The professor was waiting until I could get myself seated and he could get on without me distracting his audience. Scarlet with embarrassment, I saw with incredible gratitude that one kind young man at the end of a row was moving up to make room for me.

Once the lecture was over, I turned to thank him. His name was Neil Clarke and it turned out that we were both in the same tutorial group. He had just left school, I was twenty-two. We became firm friends, a friendship which lasted for life and ended in second marriages to one another when we had both been widowed. But at that stage he hadn't even met Sonia, his beloved first wife, and I, of course, was hopelessly in love with John.

Neil was a Catholic too, which cemented the bond between us. He was one of the young friends from my year invited to a party at my home to meet my parents; as a Catholic Neil ticked Daddy's box. We danced decorously in the living room to the music of gramophone records: Bing Crosby, Frank Sinatra and Dean Martin. Later in the month a small social get-together was held in the college. I invited John who must have felt rather out of things in a crowd of teenagers.

John and I were still having regular dates, mostly occasions on which he took me out to dinner in London restaurants or we met up with some of his friends. It was on 26th November when we were sitting in a quiet bar in a square in Soho that he asked me to marry him.

To say I was astonished would be no exaggeration. Rather than expressing my rapture, which was considerable, I said, 'Why on earth didn't you ask me before I started at university?'

'Because I want you to finish.'

We went into a nearby church to say a prayer and he bought me a holy picture.

On the back of it he wrote a message: 'God bless you, darling'. That was the very first time he had used any such term of endearment. I still have the picture.

After that he drove me back to Hornchurch. As it happened, Mummy was away in Glasgow visiting Granny. I have a suspicion that John chose this particular day on the principal of divide and conquer. He knew that tackling Daddy on his own would be easier than breaking the news to both my parents.

When we arrived my father had already gone up to bed. I rushed upstairs, 'Daddy, John has asked me to marry him!'

Muttering, 'Why do these things always have to happen to me when your mother is in Scotland?' Daddy flung on his dressing gown and tied the cord. He came downstairs, shook John's hand and produced a bottle of whiskey.

John had a history with whiskey, he told me afterwards. As a young medical student, the first time he had invited a girl to a formal dance he had gone to collect her from her father's home where he had a considerable wait before his date appeared.

Nervously, he accepted a large whiskey from her father. The wait went on and he accepted another and then a third. By the time the girl came down ready to leave John was unable to stand up. The date had to be cancelled and he could never really bear the taste of whiskey after that. But whiskey was my father's drink and John was not about to offer any resistance to his invitation. The discussion went on and Daddy explained to him several times that no such important matter could be dealt with in the absence of Mummy.

It was decided that John could come back the following evening when Mummy would be there. One thing my father was prepared to say without consultation: 'No wedding until you finish your degree, understand that!'

Poor Daddy – I never heard anyone argue about it, but somehow or other Mummy, as soon as she heard the news, was planning our wedding for the long university vacation the following summer. My parents were already very fond of John and delighted to welcome him into the family. That first evening she asked him for his home address in preparation for announcing the engagement in *The Times, The Telegraph* and the *Irish Independent.*

Slightly panicked, John drew me aside and asked if I could get my mother to hold off for a couple of days so that he could contact people in Ireland – among whom, I heard later from Anne Toal, was an Irish girlfriend who was in the habit of giving him a weekly call at the Woolwich hotel where he and Anne were both billeted as assistants in the same practice.

My first year at King's seemed to fly by. My parents had very good friends who had a jewellery shop in the Burlington Arcade. John and I went to choose an engagement ring there, and their niece Kathleen, who would become a lifelong friend, helped me choose. John could only afford a Victorian gold band with a small sapphire surrounded by diamonds but promised me that he would be finding a better one for me in the future. I never wanted another one; I wear it to this day.

My university contemporaries were a little surprised when I told them about our engagement. The other six girls in my year were all interesting – one became the first woman judge appointed to the High Court of Calcutta, another who became a particular friend was Anne Curnow, the baby of our year at age seventeen, who went on to have an enormously successful career at the criminal Bar and eventually became a Treasury silk and a Bencher of our Inn of Court.

Very early on I chose the path to becoming a barrister. Our dean, Professor Graveson, he who expected me to be a steadying influence on the younger girls, was a Bencher at Gray's; if you wanted to go to the Bar from King's it was inevitable that you applied to Gray's.

There are four Inns of Court and membership of one of them is the only path to becoming a barrister. The others are Middle Temple, Inner Temple and Lincoln's. Before my engagement to John I had applied to Gray's and been accepted.

In those days students for the Bar exams had to 'keep' twelve terms. There were four dining terms a year in the Inns each lasting a few weeks. Keeping a term involved attending dinner at the Inn on three occasions during one of the terms. The custom derived from the Middle Ages when the Inns were just that – hostelries where student lawyers could meet and be trained by practising advocates.

So, in my day, eating your total of thirty-six dinners was just as essential a preliminary to attaining one's goal as were the Bar exams themselves. There were elaborate procedures for dining: students at the long tables were separated into 'messes' of four; there was a strictly observed and complicated process by which your mess toasted the mess below you and the mess above you, so that you learned the names of eleven other members of the Inn. Any breach of the rules – such as getting someone's name wrong during the toasting or toasting the upper mess before they had toasted you – could be punished afterwards by bringing a complaint before the Senior in Hall. Appropriate dress was essential. Even the faintest grey stripe on the suit worn under the compulsory gown could bring a charge that the unfortunate male was 'wearing a white coat'.

But no charge could be brought until the benchers had left the top table for their brandy and liqueurs in their quarters behind the dining room. And even then no one could leave until the Senior in Hall had given permission to smoke, which had to be sought by the Junior in Hall. Students anxious to get away would bang the tables and shout 'Up Junior' but the unfortunate Junior might have to make his/her application several times before Mr or Madam Senior would condescend to hear it.

Allegations of impropriety would then be argued before the Senior, with the accused being given an opportunity to defend themselves. The judgment would then be delivered and if punishment were to be imposed it could be that the defeated protagonist had to sing a song, give a recital on the piano, recite a poem or – failing all else – purchase a decanter of port for the victorious mess. This was not such an expensive punishment as one might imagine since Good Queen Bess had enjoyed herself so much on one visit to the Hall that she had granted Gray's permanent exemption from paying tax on port, with the result that a decanter cost four shillings and sixpence in my time. I have no idea if that exemption still applies.

It all sounds a bit of nonsense nowadays but, at a time when the Bar was a small community – under 1300 practising barristers in England and Wales when I was a student in contrast to the current estimate of 16,500! – it meant that you came to know most people in your own Inn. The charges gave an opportunity for lessons in basic advocacy too.

At my first dinner, I was kindly escorted by John

Prosser, a third year student, and we shared our mess with two elderly gentlemen whose names I shall never forget: Hollinghurst and Pirie. In those days the Inn was like a club – men retired from other professions would join, not with any intention of reading for the exams but simply as an opportunity to seek congenial company.

When they saw my surname on the list one of them said, 'McAleer is an unusual name. Do you have any family member in the RAF?' I was delighted to be able to inform him that a cousin of Daddy's was 'quite high up in the RAF, a squadron leader'. They looked suitably impressed. When the Benchers left for their post prandial nourishment the Inn's Butler came to our mess with an invitation from the Benchers that our new friends join them.

A friend of John Prosser's came over and said, 'Goodness, you two were in distinguished company tonight.' It turned out that Hollinghurst and Pirie were both Air Chief Marshals. That story made its way into *Graya,* our house magazine and I was never allowed to forget it.

Poor John had a distinguished career, taking silk and then being appointed a circuit judge, but he blotted his copybook in 1993 when he was sentencing a fifteen-year-old boy who had raped a schoolgirl and directed that the boy pay £500 so that his victim could 'have a good holiday'.

This was widely reported and criticised in the media, the Court of Appeal eventually deciding that the sentence had been 'unduly lenient' and replacing it with two years detention. I can't help feeling that the poor girl would have enjoyed the holiday better, but that's probably why I never made the judiciary myself. The fuss did die down and John's career did not suffer.

I was able to keep my first few terms before my marriage. Despite all the distractions, I did manage to pass my first year university exams. Poor Neil was organising Student Cross, the annual Easter pilgrimage to Walsingham, that year and as a result he failed criminal law and had to spend the whole of his vacation studying to re-take, while simultaneously earning himself some pocket money harvesting peas for a cannery at a farm near where he lived.

Before the end of the academic year there was one necessary adjustment to make: I had to inform the Registrar of the College about my impending change of surname. He was a very formal gentleman, more than intimidating when he looked at me over his *pince nez,* fountain pen suspended, and intoned disapprovingly, 'I did not think you could do that.'

I had a moment of sheer panic. I knew of course that some women's colleges did not allow their undergraduates to marry, but it had not until then occurred to me that King's might impose the same restriction.

'Do – what?' I faltered.

'Find a more impossible name than McAleer,' was the answer. I sighed with relief.

- CHAPTER FOUR -
JOHN

My parents were famous for their parties – particularly their annual New Year's Eve shindig which was legendary and a direct consequence of our Glasgow origins. As children in Scotland, Oonagh and I had absorbed that New Year was even more important than Christmas – for all I know, that is still the case in Scotland.

Preparations for the big day included a meticulous spring clean of the entire flat. All the scrubbing and polishing resulted in a spotless environment in which to celebrate the upcoming change of date. The idea was that whatever you were doing on January 1st, wherever you were, would foreshadow the course of your life for the whole of the remainder of that year.

Vast quantities of food would be prepared: scones, cake and meringues, a ham with its mustard and brown sugar coating studded with cloves, various salads, there might even be a turkey. All this because of Hogmanay – New Year's Eve.

Oonagh and I would be dressed in our best, our hair shining from Granny's application of vinegar to the rinsing water after the shampooing, our frocks starched and immaculate, shoes polished and party pieces rehearsed to perfection by the aunties.

By the time the day itself arrived we could hardly bear the excitement: Granny would be hosting her party of the year. Before it could take place our 'first foot' had to be carefully chosen: tradition insisted that the first person to come through the front door should be a tall, dark, handsome man.

Perish the thought that it might, by some oversight, turn out to be, for example, our short, sandy-haired Aunt Kathleen! It appeared that a man who fitted the appropriate description would bring luck throughout the new year, where my poor aunt would have had precisely the opposite effect.

Mummy's cousin Jack was usually Granny's chosen one. He must carry with him a bottle of whiskey, a few pieces of coal and some cake to ensure that we would want for nothing over the coming months. Granny, the family and our guests would see him out into the cold before the clocks began to strike twelve, at the last stroke he would ring the door bell and bring in the year for us. There were years where a particularly welcome first-footer like Jack would be so much in demand that he would have to ring several door bells.

At Mummy's parties in Hornchurch, slightly bemused English guests found themselves being instructed on the vital necessity of our first foot to be a handsome man bringing the appropriate gifts with him. John fitted the bill perfectly.

In England as in Glasgow the hospitality would be more than generous. And we would all end up singing round the piano or listening appreciatively to someone reciting a favourite poem or telling some (suitable) jokes. In my teens I was the pianist and the songs would go on for hours, some as solos, some in chorus, never finishing until about two or three in the morning.

On one such occasion, when the family believed that all the guests had said their farewells, I was helping to turn out the lights on the way to my bed when I found a rather inebriated Glaswegian friend of Daddy's talking into our telephone. 'And-furr-therr-more,' he was enunciating with the care of someone who had clearly over-indulged, 'you can KEEP your bloody taxi!'

As soon as our engagement had taken place, Mummy fixed a date and began to plan a party to which close friends and family were to be invited to celebrate it. Inevitably, as no one in John's family lived in England, that meant ourselves, some of our friends and some of John's.

Anne and Frank were included of course; Anne arrived clutching a large cuddly toy rather than the more usual gift of wine or chocolates. Seeing Mummy looking slightly bewildered, Anne explained that her present was 'for John's brother-in-law'. That was the first time any of us had realised the incongruity of the future relationship between Mike, not yet two years old, and John in his thirties.

The Keefe family were great friends of ours. We had first met when Oonagh and I had arrived in Hornchurch. Dorothy and Catherine were a bit older than me, Denis was exactly my age and John a year older than Oonagh. They had four younger step brothers. Their father, also a GP, was a Catholic colleague of Daddy's with a practice in Romford, close to Hornchurch.

My first memory of John Keefe, then aged about six, is of him crawling under the grand piano to get away from me at a children's party. Time had not really improved our relationship. When I opened the door to them on the evening of the party, John said: 'Congratulations, Maureen – I've seen that look in your eye for some time, and I was afraid it was going to be me!'

It was obvious to me, as her sister, that Oonagh had been in love with John Keefe for some time. As Daddy's closest friend, his father Denis was invited to propose a toast to the health of the engaged couple. Raising his glass, he began: 'I have known *Oonagh* since she was a small child…' Everyone started to laugh because it was clear that he had set his heart on Oonagh as a daughter-in-law.

In fact, when John Keefe qualified in medicine a couple of years later his father gave him a sum of money to buy a new suit 'for interviews'. John waited until his father was having a bath, knocked on the bathroom door and shouted, 'You know that money you gave me for a new suit? Well, I've spent it on an engagement ring.'

I don't think Denis minded at all.

As I have already mentioned, Anne and Frank lived with John in the same hotel in Woolwich. It was a fairly dismal Victorian building, set well back from the road and surrounded by trees, with a cheerless interior decor, the kind of place one could well imagine might be haunted. The cook there resented the request that she should provide fish on Fridays for the three

Catholics. One Friday the taste of the white sauce in which the unidentifiable fish had been served was so horrible that Frank and Anne refused to eat it. But poor John was hungry and managed to swallow it, with the consequence that he became violently ill. It was discovered that the cook had thickened the sauce with some cleaning powder rather than flour, whether by accident or design. John could have died of food poisoning, but thankfully he had a strong constitution.

Many of the residents in the hotel were army personnel – the existence of the barracks at Woolwich ensured that a number of officers and their wives stationed there would use it as their base.

Before John had proposed to me one of the army wives suggested one evening that about a dozen or so of her fellow guests might like to join her in a session of table turning. This would mean that they all sat around a large table attempting to communicate with the 'other world' through some sort of spiritual agency.

Letters of the alphabet were placed around the table and each participant placed one finger on an upturned beer glass in the middle of it. The idea was that the hostess would attempt to contact some 'spirit' and see whether or not the other world had any message for anyone present.

John did not like the sound of it at all, believing it to be at best sheer stupidity, at worst a risky business, if you believe in another world, which he did. But Anne and Frank persuaded him to join in, and he told me about it after we had become engaged.

To begin with, he told me, there was a lot of larking about – the spiritualist calling 'Is anybody there?' in vain, and the participants trying to shove the glass so that they could get a pretend 'message'. But things changed after a few minutes. John described the glass as beginning to have a momentum of its own, not responding to any physical push. Shortly after this the glass went to the letters of its first word and spelled out YES.

'Who is the message for?'

JOHN

What is the message?

BRING MAUREEN HOME.

In Tipperary in John's childhood that expression was used about someone who was to get married. John was quite shaken by what had happened and broke up the meeting by leaving the table. At that stage Anne and Frank knew of my existence, but John and his friends were all so much older than me that they had never imagined he could have any intention to marry me. As I have already mentioned, Anne's theory was that I must have an older sister in whom he was interested.

She and Frank were pretty shaken too, as they could feel that the glass was moving of its own volition. They could not possibly have moved it themselves because there were so many others with a finger on it. That was the end of spiritualism as far as John was concerned.

But he had at least one other experience difficult to explain unless he had something of the quality the Irish call 'fey'. On his first voyage with the RNVR, medical officer on a naval supply ship in the Far East, he dreamt that he was back home in Tipperary. In the dream he heard his father call out in the middle of the night. All the family were there and hurried to his bedroom where he was discovered to have suffered a massive heart attack which turned out to be fatal.

His father had been in robust health when John had left Ireland. When he woke up from the dream, he could not shake off his feelings of grief and told himself not to be so ridiculous.

Communications were extremely slow in those times and it was a few days later when the captain of his ship sent for him to break the news that his father had died suddenly. The ship was so crowded that some of the ratings had to sleep on the ammunition racks rather than bunks. There was nowhere to grieve alone; many times he told me of his regret that he and his father had no relationship – the youngest of eleven siblings, he had lost his mother when he was eight years old.

Eventually, when he first got leave and returned to his family, he discovered that his father's death had taken place exactly as in his dream, save only that he was absent. Whenever he talked about having no relationship with his father I would remind him that he had heard his father call him from the other side of the world.

He could only remember that, after his mother's death, his father – a busy and successful cattle man with several farms – seemed to John so busy that there was no room in his life for him, leaving him to be brought up by a succession of housekeepers. He had six surviving older brothers and a sister, Mary, just a year older than him.

Often, when he came home from the local village

school, his supper would be just a cold potato in his hand. He was ashamed to play games with other boys because his jersey had so many holes in it that he would try to hide by pressing his elbows to his sides rather than chase the ball.

James, the second son of the family, was always kind to him but the whole family were kept busy on a farm where they produced everything they needed: meat, flour, milk, cream, butter, cheese, eggs, fruit and vegetables. The only things they needed to buy were sugar and salt.

John had his own job from when he was five years old. He was responsible for taking a heifer to the local butcher once a week, his sole companion the farm sheep dog; in truth it was the dog who was in charge of the whole expedition.

In a crowded home, John shared a bed with James at a time when the only illumination in the hours of darkness was afforded by candles. One night John woke in the small hours and decided to light a candle, with the help of a match and a handy piece of paper on the dressing table. James woke up and identified the paper as a five pound note, an enormous sum in those days, but he never reproached John about it.

James liked to smoke and would send John with the money to buy him a packet of woodbines. John's great pal was Tommy Quigley, the farmhand, who had a large number of children and was anything but well off as a result. Every time he bought cigarettes for James, John would extract one from the pack and give it to Tommy, believing that James would never notice that it was missing. James, who probably thought that John was smoking them himself, never remarked on it.

As I said, the Quigleys had a large family. John told me that some of the younger members may have actually been born to Tommy's daughters as a result of affairs they had with local young men, but they were all accepted happily into his brood. When I was having my babies, Moll Quigley was frequently held up to me as a model of fortitude. 'Moll would be snagging turnips in the field and say to my father that she had to go inside for a bit, give birth to another baby and come back snagging turnips.'

I never managed to come anywhere near that high standard.

We would take the children over to Tipperary to spend our summer holiday on the farm belonging to Paddy, one of John's bachelor brothers. On one of those holidays John was told that Tommy was dying in the local hospital; we went to visit him.

Tommy's eyes were closed and he was breathing with considerable difficulty. When John identified himself, Tommy whispered, 'John – little John,' and there were tears in John's eyes.

When he was eleven he was sent to a boarding school from which all his older brothers had run away. He stuck it out, but was regularly beaten there and would describe how all the boys rushed over to the classroom radiator first thing in the morning to warm their hands before the lessons, where the inevitable strappings began.

John often talked about his mother, who had died at the age of fifty, having given birth to eleven children by the time she was forty-two. She never had the assistance of a doctor or a nurse, the local 'handywoman' would be called in to assist with a birth, in the absence of any form of analgesic; that was the way of it in Tipperary in those days. She and John's father had to suffer the loss of three of their children in infancy, but that was only to be expected at the time.

His mother was always called on when a friend or neighbour had a serious burn: she had some herbal remedy for burns which everyone in the locality relied on. John remembered her as looking very pale and believed that she might have died of anaemia, which would have been unsurprising in view of her obstetric history.

The night she died the family were reciting the rosary, a daily observance. They heard their father cry out. John was carried upstairs by James and instructed to kiss her, even though he was terrified and grief stricken.

He remembered one particular incident from his childhood and it continued to affect him throughout his life: at about five years old he had opened the door to a tramp and taken it upon himself to send the poor man away. When his mother realised what had happened, she told him to run after the tramp and invite him for a cup of tea and some food in the kitchen, explaining to John that you never turn your back on someone in need.

Decades later we acquired a pet tramp of our own. Frank called himself a gardener, but relieved us of some of our best plants, inherited from the keen gardeners who sold us Larkfield, no doubt for sale to his other clients, confident that John and I wouldn't notice. We did but John never challenged Frank about it.

In the colder months of winter it became Frank's habit to take up residence in our garage for a couple of weeks or so at a time. No doubt he had other garages and slept in them in rotation. One Christmas it happened to be our turn. When one of the children reported that Frank was in residence John invited him in to give him a meal in the kitchen. We were all in the sitting room watching some seasonal programme on TV; John brought Frank in after his meal for a cup of tea and a slice of Christmas cake.

Frank settled himself near the fire and, one by one, the children moved away from the pungent smell the heat was generating. Eventually, even Grouse, our springer spaniel, had had enough and moved away too. The children never forgot that particular Christmas.

Once he had lost his mother, John never had any celebration for a birthday, not even for his 21st when he was a medical student in Dublin; the date simply meant nothing to him. The summer before we became engaged Mummy had somehow discovered when it was and gave a surprise family dinner party for his 32nd birthday, complete with a cake baked by herself and celebratory wine.

John already adored Mummy. In fact, he told me later that when you were considering marrying a girl it was a good idea to check out her mother to see how the prospective bride might look after the passage of years.

So I suspect he might have been in love with Mummy before he began to be in love with me!

- CHAPTER FIVE - THE WEDDING

John had no guile. At some stage he asked me for a photograph. I booked an appointment with a studio photographer, and for the first time in my life it would not be shared with Oonagh. Naturally I told him I would like a photo of him in return.

When he gave me his I asked, 'Who was the girl?'

He looked at me in genuine astonishment. 'How did you know?' he asked.

I pointed out that three sides of the picture had a white border. This was a bit of a giveaway.

Decades later, after John's death, I was invited to contribute a weekly column to a Catholic newspaper, a job which lasted for twelve years. The editor wanted a photograph of me for the column. I had to tell him that the only recent ones I could find had me clutching a golf club, a glass or a grandchild.

Early in the December after our engagement, I received the one letter John ever wrote to me:

Not being able to find my book on letter writing I'm afraid I shall have to depend on my own literary endeavours. However, now that I've incriminated myself to the extent of putting a ring on your finger, I can afford to take a few extra chances. The time at the moment seems to be divided into two parts – when I'm seeing you and when I'm not, and the latter is not by any means good.

I still have the letter and I am very glad I kept it. This was the only letter I ever received from him throughout our nine months of being engaged and the forty-seven years of our marriage. To be fair, John had good grounds for his reluctance to write. He had been born left-handed and had it literally beaten out of him at school, until he learned to write with his right hand as all Irish children were expected to do.

Also, John and I, once married, never spent a night apart unless one of us was in hospital (with the exception of a pretty disastrous weekend when he was invited to play golf with a few hard-drinking Irish friends. He couldn't get home quickly enough, and told me he had done all his adventuring when he was a sailor).

I keep that letter with the only postcard he sent me. The previous summer Jimmy and I stayed with our Uncle Willie in Dublin, where John was on holiday too with his friend Joe, subsequently to be our best man.

It became painfully obvious during that holiday that Jimmy had been given strict instructions by Daddy not to leave me alone with John on any account. He trailed along after us wherever we went and frankly made himself a perfect nuisance. That postcard was an invitation to go for a drive into the country and made it plain that fourteen-year-old Jimmy's company would be less than welcome.

I could see that Jimmy was taking Daddy's admonitions seriously and enjoying his position as chaperon, but that afternoon a lucky solution to the problem presented itself. The smell of cigarette smoke in the bathroom he and I shared in the guest house was unmistakable. Jimmy did not need more than a hint of what I might report back to Daddy to climb down and make himself scarce for a few hours.

To be honest, Daddy's attitude to John during the period when we were 'doing a line', as dating was called in Ireland, and even after our engagement, made things very difficult for me. Daddy's rule was that I was to be home in Hornchurch by 10.30pm without fail. John's friends, in their thirties, found it laughable that a night out in London had to finish for us by 9.45pm at the very latest. Unsurprisingly, John resented the situation.

I would persuade him into his car as soon after 9.45pm as I could, but it was often a few minutes later. Tense with nerves, my fists clenched, I would count the landmarks along the familiar route home praying that we would be there by the deadline. Very often we were not. John and I would often not be speaking by that point.

Daddy would be waiting, ready to welcome John with all his charm, and he and John would have a friendly conversation. Once John had driven off, however, I knew what was coming. 'What time do you call this?' Daddy would demand, drawing his eyebrows together as an indication of his displeasure.

Sometimes I cried myself to sleep. It says a lot about John that he didn't allow himself to react to Daddy's quite unreasonable attitude. I don't think Mummy approved of it, but she would never have taken my side against Daddy's. At least we had the wedding to look forward to.

During the Dublin holiday John had taken me to a very grand hotel in order to introduce me to Father Bobby, one of his two priest brothers, together with brother James and his wife Tesha. I had no idea of the significance of this occasion at the time, only realising later that he wanted his family to approve of me as a future wife. At that stage I believed John to be the 'typical Irish bachelor' depicted by Daddy.

No other member of John's family had left Ireland to live elsewhere, never mind giving any thought to marriage with an 'English' girl, and I know they must all have been worrying about him, the youngest member of their clan.

Luckily, I got on with them all very well. Father Bobby soon established that I was a convent-educated practising Catholic, which must have been a considerable relief. He had spent the war years as a missionary in Nigeria, so chatting about my parents' experience there also gave us a pleasant connection. They were, like my paternal grandparents, a farming family. Bobby only told me years later that they had all assumed I had a dowry or John would not have considered marrying me.

It was decided that Bobby and Father Willie, who was on leave from missionary work in Nigeria, would conduct the wedding between them. In those days it was not possible for priests to con-celebrate Mass so Bobby was to marry us and Father Willie to say the Mass. The two brothers were very different characters. Bobby soon invited me to use his Christian name; Willie never did.

In fact, when John and I celebrated our twenty-fifth wedding anniversary it was Willie who was saying the Mass for all our family and friends.

I think only he, on such an occasion, could have kicked off his sermon with 'Only a priest knows how difficult married life can be!'

The poor man had heard so much about the difficulties in the confessional that it was inconceivable to him that two people could be as happily married as we were. It was after that Mass that John asked Willie if I could drop the 'Father' as we had known one another and been related for twenty-five years. Willie just pretended that he hadn't heard him.

But he was a loving uncle to our children and generous with his gifts of African artefacts whenever he came to stay with us during his leaves. He was an avid collector, particularly interested in clocks, glass and china. When staying with us he liked to take one of our daughters into the local department store where he would head for the floor where these fragile objects could be found. Unfortunately he was a large man and a bit clumsy; in the confined passages between the display cabinets he would frequently brush against some delicate object with the child in question having to make a grab to prevent it crashing to the floor.

Once when our eldest daughter Maureen was about five years old, Willie wanted to see the TV news and asked her to switch it on. 'We have to ask Mummy if we want to do that,' she told him.

'Oh well,' he said. 'Mummy's the boss.'

Maureen was anxious to put him right. 'No,' she explained. 'Daddy's the boss. But he lets her do the bossing.'

Quite an interesting analysis of a relationship for a child of her age.

When he retired from his work in Nigeria to Cork in Ireland John and I would visit him when we were on holiday there. He had never driven a car himself but enjoyed going out with us to have a meal in a restaurant in the city. He would be our guide through the busy streets, but could never understand John refusing to follow his directions if the way he indicated had a 'No Entry' sign.

'Ah, hang it all,' he would protest. 'Isn't that the only way to get there?'

One summer we were travelling through Ireland for a golfing holiday with our great friends, Mary and Jim MacNamara and called in on him. I happened to be wearing golfing trousers, Mary happened to be wearing a skirt. Willie followed me into the kitchen where I was putting the kettle on to make a cup of tea.

'Mary MacNamara,' he said. 'A *lady* to her fingertips!'

I'm afraid it was my trousers which had upset him.

John's family came over for the wedding, of course. I think it was the first time any of them had ever been out of Ireland, apart from the two priests. My parents had been planning the event with the greatest care. Daddy, in particular, had been fussing about every detail, but things did not exactly go as they should have done.

John was supposed to spend the day with his family and have his stag night that evening, as was the custom at the time. Sadly, the death of the father of his partner in the practice occurred that day. John had to cope with the surgeries and home visits on his own and only arrived at about 10.00pm – no chance of a drink with his friends as had been planned.

But worse was in store: when the two priests called our parish priest to confirm Daddy's arrangements for the following day, it turned out that Canon Van Meenan, who had been on a pilgrimage to Lourdes, had been unable to return due to a general strike in France which was disrupting train and ferry services.

The priest who was deputising for him in his absence denied any knowledge of a wedding the following day and actually seemed to disbelieve that Bobby and Willie were genuine priests. He adamantly refused to consider allowing the wedding to take place.

Daddy was incandescent but powerless. A new plan had to be made immediately. The priest in an adjoining parish was a friend and unhesitatingly offered his church as our venue. It would mean, of course, that guides would have to be placed outside St Joseph's to re-direct the wedding guests, many of them non-Catholics who would have found the whole situation at best amusing, at worst scandalous.

Just when Daddy was choosing between a heart attack and a nervous breakdown, we had a phone call from our parish priest who had managed to cross the Channel after all. So the wedding could go ahead on the basis described in the engraved wedding invitations.

In those days Catholic weddings were always timed to take place in the morning. If we were to receive Holy Communion we had to be fasting from midnight and 10.00am was the appointed time. With Daddy's threat that if I were not dressed and ready by 9.30am he would, 'go and marry John Mullally himself', I was ready at the appointed hour.

Dear Mr Sunnick, the uniformed chauffeur who had always taken Oonagh and me to and from our convent school at the beginnings and ends of term, had witnessed my tears on many of those return journeys and tactfully appeared to have been unaware of them. He had polished his ancient limousine to unprecedented brilliance and his own broad smile was reflected in the results of his hard work.

We were on time, of course. Daddy would have permitted nothing less. On the way to the church he predicted gloomily that I would 'never finish' my degree. Oonagh was the principal bridesmaid, Jimmy a groomsman in hired morning dress to match the wear of all the other men present who owned their own, Mike aged two-and-a-half was resplendent in a new white suit. One of the wedding photos reveals him holding Oonagh's hand and contentedly snacking on the flowers in her bouquet.

At the foot of the altar, when we were really married, we turned to look at one another – my first thought as a married woman was, 'he's wearing the wrong tie'. John's best man Joe, even more nervous than John himself, had failed to notice that he was wearing his bright blue 'going away' tie rather than the one which completed the morning dress. But it was a foretaste of what was to come. John was never able to work out what garment 'went' with another, it was never important to him.

The wedding reception went well but seemed to be over in a flash. After the speeches had been made, the toasts drunk and the wedding cake cut, Mummy whispered, 'You and John should leave soon so that everyone can start enjoying themselves.'

Incredibly, that was how weddings were in those days. Our guests had seen us off by lunchtime. It didn't matter that John's family had come all the way from Tipperary or that Granny and the aunties had come down from Scotland. Changed into our 'going away' outfits in the hotel, we were given an emotional send-off by our nearest and dearest, and left to drive away to our honeymoon in the early afternoon. I was wearing a pale blue Jaeger suit with a little hat entirely composed of white feathers, which I really loved.

We had by no means reached the end of our troubles. As I have already mentioned there was a general strike in France. Ambitiously, for those days, we had booked to spend three weeks there. Currency regulations restricted each of us to £50 and there was an additional allowance for petrol for the car, but I can't remember how much that was.

Anyway, thanks to all the drama on the wedding eve, John and I somehow or other managed to forget to bring our allowances. We had booked a night in a hotel in Kent on the way to the ferry, but luckily realised our omission on emerging from the Blackwall Tunnel. We phoned the hotel, where the wedding reception was being enjoyed in our absence, and told Daddy that John had left the allowances on the dining room sideboard at home. The owner of the reception hotel, a family friend, kindly offered to meet us outside the tunnel bringing the vital currency.

Great. Except that we discovered next day on our

way to the ferry that he had only brought £50, leaving the other £50 and the car allowance behind. That might have been the point where anyone with any sense would have given considerable thought to whether France was going to be the ideal destination for us. But we were staying with the lovely French family I had spent three months with a couple of years previously, and we decided that if our money wouldn't stretch far enough I could always borrow some from them to be repaid later.

- CHAPTER SIX -
THE HONEYMOON

This did not get off to a good start. When we disembarked in France John, who had never driven on the right, immediately took the car into the wrong lane. A French lorry driver made an appropriate comment, fortunately unintelligible to John who was never a linguist. We were meant to be heading south. Mummy had kindly lent us her map of France, but I am not very good at map reading. In my defence it must be said that we were aiming to go through Paris and Mummy's map pre-dated the Périphérique, the ring road around the city, with the consequence that we got totally lost and ended up going north, arriving accidentally at Étretat, a small seaside resort on the Normandy coast, both exhausted and John a little annoyed.

I wasn't too pleased myself. It had been unbearably hot that day and we had opened all the windows of the car to their fullest extent. At one point, my lovely little feathered hat, which had been on the back windowsill, flew out of the car of its own volition. 'Stop, please stop!' I begged, but to no avail. That was the last I saw of the hat.

Eventually John stopped the car, took a look at the map himself, and decided that we would find a little hotel and book in for the night, hopefully sorting ourselves out in the right direction the following morning. When we entered the restaurant for dinner a very friendly fellow-guest, a French lady, found out that I could speak the language and asked me if we were on our honeymoon. I hadn't thought it was that obvious and was a bit surprised, but I had to admit it.

However, she insisted on having a long chat and wondered where we were going next. I explained that we were heading south. Well, why were we not going to spend a few days in Paris? Even I knew that Paris in August would be practically deserted and very hot. 'Oh no, you are absolutely wrong about that,' she told me. 'Paris in August is wonderful. I have friends in the couture houses and I could arrange for you to have a look.' I told her about our currency problem. She told me that Paris was definitely the answer, and that she knew the most delightful little hotel which was really cheap, and could recommend so many things we could do inexpensively if only we were to spend some time there.

John naturally had no idea what all this conversation was about, but the lady insisted on introducing both of us to her husband, explaining to him that we were on our honeymoon, and it must include Paris. So I translated everything for John's benefit.

He was extremely doubtful about her whole proposition. But, she explained, as it happened, she and her husband were planning to return to Paris the following day. What could be more convenient for us than to give them a lift – she would be able to solve all our problems with the Périphérique and act as a perfect guide for our sojourn. John was still reluctant, but, for me, not having to read the map was such a relief. I persuaded John that her idea was a good one.

So the following morning we set off, my friend giving excellent directions, when we stopped for lunch her husband kindly paid the bill.

As we reached the outskirts of Paris, however, her manner changed. '*À gauche! À droit*!' she began to snap, losing her temper if John failed to follow her instructions immediately. Eventually we reached her destination, the block of apartments where she and her husband lived.

Madame and Monsieur exited the car and collected their luggage from our boot; she explained in a rush that they couldn't invite us in because they had been away for a few weeks and the apartment would be in disorder. She then gave directions to a cheap hotel nearby and that was the last we saw of her.

Of course we had been comprehensively taken advantage of. The strike meant that the couple had no means of returning to Paris, she had devised her scheme on realising how naive I was. John had been deeply suspicious all along, but I was the one who understood French. On the plus side, it was an experience which made me realise how very much wiser in worldly ways my husband was, which was at least a good foundation for our married relationship in the future.

Needless to say, the recommended hotel, though certainly cheap, was really frightful; we couldn't get away from it fast enough the following day. Somehow I began to be able to read the map better and we did find ourselves heading south.

Our next objective was to reach Châteauroux, the town where I had spent three happy months with my French family, on an exchange with their daughter Françoise. I had promised John that I would ask them for a loan to supplement our meagre ration of francs. On our leisurely way there we spent our nights in very basic accommodation, dining frugally and having picnic lunches.

John's partner, Seán and his wife Joyce had given us a magnificent picnic hamper as a wedding present, fitted with plates, cups, saucers, drinking glasses and cutlery for four. Unsurprisingly it weighed a ton, but it did come in handy for the picnic meals. John had also brought a little kettle and a primus stove so that we could have a cup of tea at our chosen spot. We purchased delicious bread, *pâtés,* salads, cheese and fruits in local markets or delicatessens.

On one unforgettable occasion the stove was nearly our complete undoing. We had stopped by a grassy bank at the top of which was a field of wheat. By some awful mischance the lighted primus tipped over, setting fire to the August tinder-dry grass which immediately spread along the bank.

'Save the picnic basket!' John shouted, with no apparent regard for my safety, as he vainly attempted to put the fire out with his sandalled bare feet.

We did get everything into the car and John drove it away from the burning undergrowth. But he was a farmer's son and, having parked the car at safe distance, he returned to the scene and somehow managed to crush the fire to ashes before it reached the wheat, scorching his poor feet in the process.

Whether as a result of that, or of the usually unappetising meals we could afford in the evenings, John developed a severe tummy upset when we had booked into yet another cheap hotel that night. He was feeling so ill that he couldn't contemplate going into the restaurant for dinner, so I ate there on my own. This did not meet with the approval of the landlady, who informed me that if we were not both buying dinner we would not be able to stay there another night.

There was one guest loo in the whole establishment and John took up semi-permanent occupation in it overnight, so we were not too popular with the other guests either. Like it or not, that meant we had to leave the next morning, even though John was still very unwell.

But we were at that stage not too far from Châteauroux and driving in the fresh air happily revived him. Françoise's father had been a consultant with his own little hospital for resident patients in the grounds of their comfortable home. In addition, he owned several farms which we used to visit on our way to see the various beautiful châteaux of the Loire nearby.

He was a lovely man, fond of teasing his wife, who longed to stop at a patisserie so that we could all enjoy one of its delicious confections. 'Patisserie!' Madame would shout, pointing at it with her plump gloved finger as we approached one. But the doctor would always pretend that he couldn't see it and drive past several of them, until he eventually gave in to her pleadings. Françoise and I would always end up in giggles, which was probably what he was aiming for.

He liked teasing me too. When I arrived in Paris I

had told the family categorically that I could never eat anything containing garlic. Their cook, Marie, married to the gardener and odd job man Henri, would produce the most fantastic meals and I soon had my favourite dishes. One day, Dr Fil said to me with a twinkle in his eye, 'Did you enjoy that, Maureen?'

'It was delicious!'

'That's the garlic in it,' he said with a smile.

When they brought Françoise to Hornchurch for her three months with us, Daddy expressed his thanks to him for the improvement in my French. He shook his shoulders in his Gallic way and said, 'Well you know your daughter – she must talk! And French was the only language on offer!'

They had come up to meet me in Paris after I had travelled overnight by the train onto the ferry.

Daddy had booked me a first-class ticket, which meant that I boarded it in Victoria Station, slept the night in my comfortable bunk and crossed the Channel without even being aware of it.

This was the first time the Fil family had been in Paris since the war ended and they had many friends there so we were lavishly entertained on each of our four nights, on one of which I was taken to the Opera. Mummy had bought me a copy of a Dior 'new look' suit for the trip which earned me many compliments from fashion conscious Frenchwomen.

Not only were the meals we had amazingly good for someone who came straight from the stringent rationing still being suffered in England, but our hosts were lovingly uncorking fine wines that had been carefully hoarded during the German occupation. Doctor Fil made great efforts to introduce me to them, but that was long before I had acquired any appreciation of good wine. He would dilute exquisite vintages with water just to persuade me to try a little sip, but to his great disappointment his kind efforts were wasted on me.

When they stayed with us in Hornchurch, Daddy took us all up to London for a meal. Walking through Soho, we came across several ladies of the night, dressed to the nines and standing close to the buildings on either side of the streets. Daddy ignored them of course. But the doctor courteously removed his hat and ceremoniously bowed to each of them in turn.

Sadly, Doctor Fil had died before John and I got married. But we were warmly welcomed by Madame and Françoise when we arrived, having been invited to stay for two nights. Marie even remembered my favourite recipes of hers and recreated them for our benefit. When I had been with them Madame had been slightly terrified of her because she would not allow Madame into the kitchen to bake the cakes which Madame really loved.

Looking back on it, I now realise that this might have been on instruction from the doctor. No doubt about it, his wife was on the comfortably rounded side and it tied in with his reluctance to encourage her liking for patisseries. Not to be deterred by the cook's refusal to let her into the kitchen, Madame had the habit of using a small cooking facility upstairs, with carefully closed blinds on the windows which were open to dispel the enticing aromas from her baking. She, Françoise and I would enjoy the results without including the doctor or even the grandparents who made up the household.

Being with them again brought back so many happy memories for me. In addition to Marie and Henri they still employed a uniformed housemaid and a cleaning lady. John kept reminding me of the purpose of our visit: we badly needed additional funds and I was supposed to be borrowing them. I kept putting the request off, very conscious that Madame was now widowed.

She might be very poor now. How could I possibly have imagined that I could ask her for money?

The whole set-up there gave no indication that Madame had fallen on hard times, but I was stubbornly refusing to listen to John's pleadings.

We spent a couple of happy days there but, when it came to the point, I simply could not overcome my scruples. To John's considerable frustration, we said our farewells to Françoise, Madame and her staff without me being able to raise the topic. Needless to say, when Madame heard about it afterwards she was most upset that I had not been able to tell her the problem, which she would have been well able to help with. But it was too late then.

Both widowed now, Françoise and I still exchange cards and news every Christmas.

Somehow we managed to last the remainder of our three weeks, living as frugally as possible. I was still not that keen on wine, but France offered nothing similar to the peach juice John had been so averse to ordering in London. He did, however, manage to introduce me to Cointreau and I would finish each evening with a small glass of the sweet liqueur.

As a result of the continuing strike it would not have

been possible to book a place on an earlier ferry. The company we had booked with were only running one a day. When we reached our ferry bound for home we had no money left at all. Luckily, we met up with some friends of mine on board. They will never know how much gratitude we felt when they offered to buy us a cup of coffee.

Looking back on it all, I can see the patience that poor John had to display in order to cope with all the disasters, most of them my fault, and the resultant worries and concerns which he must have had. If the honeymoon was to be any indication of what our ensuing marriage was to be like, he might reasonably have had serious doubts about the wisdom of his choice of a wife.

But he never said anything about that.

- CHAPTER SEVEN - MARRIED LIFE BEGINS

We were home at last, and home was to be a rented semi-detached property in Eltham, South London, not too far away from Welling where John's practice was. I think we were paying four pounds ten shillings a month for it.

In the run-up to our wedding, Daddy had announced several times that he would not agree to us living in rented accommodation. He only reluctantly changed his mind when he heard that John's partner Seán and his wife Joyce were planning to move out of the surgery house and sell it to John as soon as they could find a property which they liked.

We considered ourselves very fortunate when Seán Coffey offered John the partnership. When his partner died, there were sixty applicants keen to replace him, such was the competition for inclusion in a GP practice at the time. Seán had interviewed most of them, but our luck was that we had met Seán and Joyce at a Christmas party in the home of mutual friends just after we had become engaged to be married.

Seán's existing partner at the time was terminally ill. Joyce told us much later that, on their way back to Welling after the party, Seán had remarked that when the time came to find a new partner, John Mullally was exactly the sort of man he would be looking for.

Before Seán made his final choice, however, John and I were invited to tea at the Coffeys' home in Welling, the ground floor of which was taken up by the two surgeries, the receptionist's desk in the front hall, filing cabinets containing all the patients' records, and a waiting room which held about fifty patients.

In the run-up to this important tea party, Anne and Frank were on hand to give us lots of advice. 'Now remember, Maureen,' Frank instructed me. 'It's "Yes, Mrs Coffey", "Thank you, Mrs Coffey", "How *right* you *are*, Mrs Coffey!".'

None of us were in any doubt that I was going to be just as important to the interview process as John was himself. Thankfully we must have made the right impression. Soon afterwards Seán made his offer to John.

The terms were a little harsh too. John was to accept that he would not be a full partner for five years, meaning that he would receive only a third of the practice income for that period.

In addition, we were to be responsible for all telephone calls apart from those taken by the receptionist when she was on duty. The NHS had only come into existence a few years previously in 1948. John was a great supporter of it. This meant that he would never again have to ask if a patient could afford the medication he or she needed.

Even after the NHS had been set up, many people who were comfortably off preferred to become private paying patients. There was no objection to this, of course, and for the majority of GPs it meant a considerable upgrade in their incomes, which was very welcome.

Many people asked John if they could become private patients, but he invariably refused their requests, explaining, 'I can't offer you anything I wouldn't do for my NHS patients.'

For my parents the introduction of the NHS imposed a financial burden. Daddy had paid for his share of the Hornchurch practice; the compensation he would get for supplying the bricks and mortar of the surgery buildings was to be deferred until his retirement. When he did retire two decades later the compensation he got was for the value of those premises at the date when the NHS had come in, not their current value.

The pension my mother had from the NHS when Daddy died was miserly. John was appalled when he discovered that her widow's pension for Daddy's twenty years in the service was less than Mummy was getting for the ten years Daddy had spent in Africa. As a result, when I began to earn money at the Bar, John's constantly repeated advice to me was, 'Put some more money in your pension.'

The trouble was that those negotiating with the government on behalf of general practitioners had badly let down the people they were supposed to be representing. I seem to recollect that GPs were paid something like twenty-five shillings a year for every patient on their list. This was to cover twenty-four hour duty every day of the year. The man who had negotiated that agreement was elevated to the House of Lords.

Dentists were in a much better position since their remuneration was paid on the basis of item of service, and as a result their incomes were so generous that some doctors took the trouble to re-qualify. In those years it was not uncommon for dentists from Australia, and other parts of the English speaking world, to come to practise in Britain for a few years in order to accumulate a handsome capital sum to take back home.

When John started he was on one-third of the practice income for five years, which meant that we had quite a financial struggle. At that time not only did the practice offer two surgeries a day Monday to Saturday, there was even one on Sunday mornings. And calls to the homes of patients were made every day and every night. Some nights there would be two or three!

Once, when I grumbled about a particular family who seemed always to be calling him out in the middle of the night, John said, 'They wouldn't call me unless they were worried. And if they're worried it's my job to go out and help them.'

At the time home births were more common than those taking place in hospital wards. John loved to deliver the babies of his patients, and had even taken an additional degree in midwifery when he had qualified as a doctor. Sadly, Seán did not share his interest and without his partner's support at times when he was off duty it was impossible for John to carry on delivering babies.

Even so, his work occupied a great deal more of his time than would be the case nowadays. In a two-partner practice, holidays had to be arranged between the GPs who would cover for one another other; John and Seán could not afford to pay for locums. Each had one half day a week, ours was Thursday. Initially, they took turns for weekends; it was a great relief when they managed to team up with another local practice with three practitioners, so that each doctor only had to work one weekend out of five.

While John was settling into his new practice I returned to my lectures and tutorials at King's, as we had planned. It was not long before we realised that I was expecting our first baby. Very considerately, the baby had decided to be born during the summer vacation in 1954. The winter of 1953/4 was a cold one and our rented home had no central heating, just the coal fire in the living room which was only lit in the evenings.

The front door was in a direct line through the hall to the back door. I remember that if we had brought snow into the house on our shoes before we left in the morning, the snow would still be frozen on the carpet by the time we got home in the evening. For want of any other source of warmth in the mornings, I developed the habit of crouching in front of the open oven door, having switched it on to maximum heat, to prepare me for the commute to college.

But I was lucky in one way, as I did not suffer from severe morning sickness. What would I have done if I had? Another piece of luck was that we all wore academic gowns to lectures and tutorials – the best maternity smock imaginable. It would have been very unusual if not unique to be a pregnant student in those days.

One of my tutors was Norman St John Stevas, later to become Lord St John of Fawlsley. He was a rather precious young man, devoted to Queen Victoria and confided in us that his most treasured possession was one of her stockings!

Once he became aware of my condition, the poor man lived in mortal dread that I would go into labour during one of his afternoon tutorials. If I fell asleep during some of them, he never attempted to disturb me.

John decided that we would not tell my parents about the baby until I was about three months pregnant, as early miscarriages are so common. So we spent our first married Christmas with them but said nothing about it. Daddy was upset when we broke the news. 'But you must have known about this for weeks!'

We had had a bit of trouble with Daddy within a couple of months of our starting on married life. At first we went to Hornchurch for lunch with the family every Sunday. Then came the week when John told me that we were going out with Anne and Frank next Sunday. As I suppose John must have anticipated, Daddy was upset and angry with me, of course. I was given to understand that Daddy expected that we would always be there for Sunday lunch and I tried to explain that to John, just hoping to keep the peace.

But Daddy had met his match in John, who told me to explain to him that we would always love to spend time with the family, but it would not be every Sunday. I half expected the sky to fall in on us, but Mummy must have persuaded him that John was not being unreasonable.

We had only been in Eltham for a couple of months when Seán and Joyce found a property which they liked. Unfortunately, it was in Sevenoaks, about half an hour's drive from the practice if the traffic was reasonable; getting to night calls was extremely inconvenient for

Seán. I think that John was in the very generous habit of taking more of the night calls than were his share because he felt sorry for Seán having to come all that way.

What it meant for us was a move into the surgery premises where I had my part to play in answering the many phone calls from patients when the receptionist was off duty. At least I was a little more sophisticated than when I had famously taken a call for my father and told him that it had been from a Mr Smith who was worried about his wife. 'But then, Daddy, he talked about some other lady called "Miss Kerridge".' I had recorded the name carefully, never having heard the word 'miscarriage' in my life, much less having any idea what it meant.

I was also too wise to fall into the terrible habit my mother had: several times, when a patient had called at the door and Daddy was out, she had raided his box of sample drugs and offered the patient something she thought would be appropriate to his or her complaint, having consulted the labelling. Daddy had to put a stop to that when patients began to ask him for 'that really good medicine I got from Mrs McAleer' and he had no idea what it was!

I had to get used to a new way of life once in the surgery premises. The house was a detached two-bedroom property with a small attic, and a downstairs waiting room for patients, which I think was a converted garage. Apart from the kitchen, the ground floor was entirely occupied by the two surgeries, no doubt intended to be the dining and sitting room. The entrance hall was the domain of the receptionist, a redoubtable lady called Mrs Wolf, ensconced behind her desk, together with large numbers of steel filing cabinets containing all the patients' records.

The only furniture we owned consisted of our bed, a kitchen table, and a magnificent suite of furniture originally designed for the Victorian Great Exhibition in 1851. It included a beautiful settee, a *chaise longue* or day bed, two matching armchairs, a nursing chair without arms and a set of six matching dining chairs, plus two footstools.

An aristocratic family had purchased it from the Exhibition and presented it to their butler on his retirement to live in Hornchurch. When he died his family put the whole set in a local auction and Mummy had snapped it up. When she gave it to us I imagine she must have had Daddy's agreement, but that didn't stop him saying, 'Nail down the furniture!' whenever John and I visited afterwards.

When Mummy had bought the furniture it was upholstered in a rather uninspiring green fabric. By the time we had acquired it the material was looking rather the worse for wear. Some years later, when we had moved to Bickley, we discovered a professional upholsterer locally and asked him to give us a quote for replacing it. I chose a striped regency-styled fabric which I thought much more appropriate to the beautiful carving of the chair frames.

A couple of days later Mr Huddle phoned me. 'You'll never guess what I found under that green material?' he asked. I braced myself for news of woodworm.

Far from it, he had uncovered the remnants of the

original upholstery, together with an elaborate pattern of buttoning on the backs of every seat. He was an old man who was justly proud of his artistry and asked if he could try to reproduce the intricate work. I knew we could not possibly afford the amount of labour involved.

'No I won't charge anything extra,' he said, 'I just want to do it for the love of it, to see if I can do the same – I've never seen anything like it. I think it must have been French originally.'

I remember that he delivered the suite just before Christmas; he was not looking at all well, but he was so happy to see our delight in his achievement. Poor Mr Huddle died within a few weeks of that delivery. He must already have been very ill when he carried out his work for the love of it.

The sad thing is that most of the suite has been lost, or scattered over the years. When we moved to Bickley we left the *chaise longue* in the surgery attic and it had disappeared when we went to look for it a few years later. The settee went to auction when we moved to a smaller house in 1996; none of the children had room for it at the time. We kept the chairs, the footstools and the dining chairs. When I moved to my apartment in Battersea in 2016 the dining chairs had to go; one went to each of the children still living in England, so I do have the pleasure of sitting on them occasionally. Luckily, I have been able to keep the three remaining chairs in my sitting room. They bring back so many memories every time I look at them.

- CHAPTER EIGHT -
WE START OUR FAMILY

We moved into the surgery in the spring of 1954. I had to concentrate on my studies for Part One of my final LL.B, while at the same time adjusting to being part-time telephonist for the practice. I would also meet many of John's lovely patients, two of whom would sit in the hall awaiting their turn with either John or Seán. This meant using two of the dining room chairs in the hall during surgery hours, the remaining four being used in both surgeries as seating for the doctors and the patients they were seeing.

Quite often all six dining chairs were in use during surgery hours. Before we acquired two for the kitchen we had a visit from the curate in our local parish. The surgeries were taking place, so I had to choose between inviting him to sit on the edge of our bed upstairs, or on the edge of the kitchen table. Dear Father Charles, who became a lifelong friend, eventually graduating to Bishop Charles, accepted a cup of tea perched on that table as though it were the most natural way in the world to receive hospitality.

By the time the twins were born, we had acquired more furniture. I recall handing Father Charles a twin and a bottle when he happened to arrive at feeding time. He accepted that with the same courteous grace. Many decades later, Bishop Charles was seated at the back of the Holy Ghost Chapel where we often went to Mass. My grandson Tommy, who was about three years old, commandeered his knee and handed him his child's prayer book, demanding 'Read it to me'. And he did.

He and John came from the same part of Ireland and were very close friends throughout their lives. When John died, Bishop Charles phoned me and said that he was coming to preside over the funeral, something I would never have dreamed of asking him to do.

During the summer of 1954, I took Part One with all my friends at King's. I said goodbye to them after the exams had finished because I had no intention of returning to the university for my final year.

Hugh's arrival in August was just what John expected. Two of his six brothers were priests, two of them bachelor farmers, two married. At the time he had many nephews but only one niece. He told me confidently that Hugh would be a boy, although there was no way to determine the gender of an unborn baby at that time. He also told me that we would be calling him Hugh, a name I was not very keen on at the time, although of course I have reason to love it now.

I thought that when the baby arrived John would be so delighted that he would be willing to let me choose the name. I would have liked to call him Thomas after my father.

But in John's family the tradition was that the eldest son should be named after his paternal grandfather, so Hugh it was, and we gave him the middle name of

Thomas.

We both delighted in him. He was a very good baby although, at times, like all babies he did have a little cry. Unfortunately, those times often coincided with the evening surgery. The receptionist Mrs Wolf, who was childless, would purse her lips disapprovingly at me and proclaim to the two patients waiting in the hall that she had never once heard Seán and Joyce's son Patrick cry like that.

It never occurred to me to leave Hugh to attend a lecture or tutorial for my final examinations. My very good friend, Anne Curnow, who subsequently became a highly respected Treasury silk, kindly copied her lecture notes for me. Another friend, who was one of my tutors, was good enough to come down to Welling to give me a free tutorial in exchange for a free meal. In addition to providing legal instruction, I remember he taught me how to mash potatoes!

I must admit that my culinary skills were almost non-existent when poor John took me on. On making my first apple tart I talked through the process step by step with Mummy over the telephone. Apple tarts were very important to Daddy and to John. Daddy would say that a meal wasn't a meal if it didn't finish with an apple tart. John would sneak down for a midnight snack if he happened to know there was any left over in the fridge.

Mummy had always been an amazing cook. Looking back, I cannot understand why I never bothered to learn from her, but I have to hang my head and admit that John's description of my cooking, while I was still a student as 'a dash for the tin opener and a tomato' was not very far from the truth. However, I soon learned that if you can read you can cook, and cookery books quickly became favourites on my bookshelf, to John's considerable relief.

My complete absence from lectures and tutorials did not escape the attention of the university authorities. I received a rather sniffy letter informing me that, if I could not see my way to attending any part of the course, my degree, should I pass the finals, would only be an 'exterior' one. That threat did not dismay me in the least. My ambition was to disprove Daddy's prediction that I would never finish: any degree would have that effect.

Thanks to my two good friends I did get a 2/2 in my LL.B the following summer. By that time I knew that I was expecting a second baby. Sadly, things did not go so smoothly with this pregnancy. When I was about twelve weeks into it we knew that something was wrong. I was ill in bed, surrounded by my parents, my sister Oonagh and her John, Seán Coffey, Anne and Frank, and John himself. All doctors, except my mother, and all arguing about what to do next.

While the seven medically qualified people were discussing this around my bed, Mummy, the only non-medic, slipped downstairs and phoned Farnborough Hospital where Hugh had been born. That was when Kenneth Seager, a new obstetrician at the hospital, came into our lives. He examined me and explained that there was no hope for the baby. He said to John, 'I am not a Catholic, but if you explain to me how to do it, I will baptise the foetus for you.'

That simple act of kindness, which meant so much

to both of us, presaged a friendship which endured over the years as our family increased. Eventually, before the birth of our youngest, Mary Rose, Kenneth himself became a Catholic. 'You've worn me down,' he explained to me. He became Mary Rose's godfather, obviously.

For the next few years we were to encounter one another on a regular basis.

On one occasion I was visiting a friend who had just given birth and we met in the corridor of the hospital. 'You here on business or pleasure?' he wanted to know.

I had to be admitted to Farnborough for the procedure. I took Hugh's photo with me and put it beside my bed. On his ward round, Kenneth would point it out and tell the members of his team how lucky I was to have Hugh. He was quite right, but I was mourning the lost baby too. I couldn't help it.

It wasn't too long before I was expecting another baby, due to arrive at the end of April 1956, when Hugh would be twenty months old. About six weeks before the anticipated date I was having one of the regular checks at the hospital when Kenneth said casually, 'Any twins in your family?'

Conscious that I had put on a lot of weight – probably due to my appetite – I owned up to the possibility that I had been overeating. There were no scans in those days but Kenneth said, 'I think we'll just take a look on an X-ray.'

I was so embarrassed, still convinced that I might have been a bit greedy. X-ray taken, Kenneth came back into the consulting room holding up two fingers, not with any intention of being rude. He then showed me his notes from my first consultation where he had written 'Query twins'. He was a very good obstetrician. 'There you are,' he said. 'You've been given back that baby you made all the fuss about losing.'

John came to collect me in the car and I told him what had happened. I was in a state of shock. 'Three babies under two!' I said. 'I can't do it – *nobody* could do it!'

But within half an hour I had changed my mind completely. I was so excited about the prospect and was asking him, 'It really is going to be twins? There can't be any mistake?'

As the due date approached, I became truly enormous. I couldn't see my feet and if I wanted to turn over in bed John had to do it for me. When I was admitted to hospital a couple of days before I was due I weighed fourteen stones. When I was discharged I weighed ten.

Nowadays, I would have been induced early on. Twins can be up to six weeks premature. I nearly failed Oonagh her final obstetrics oral exam because the examiner asked her about common features associated with a twin pregnancy. 'Twins can be born up to six weeks early,' she replied, 'but they can go to term.' The examiner glared at her and told her how long he had been an obstetrician, assuring her that no twin pregnancy in his long experience had gone to term. Oonagh opened her mouth to tell him about me, thought better of it, and passed the exam.

I was terrified of the matron at Farnborough, having had a bit of a run in with her when I was being supervised giving Hugh his first bath. Because of Michael I was already an expert in bathing babies. 'You've had a baby before!' she said accusingly. I don't think she was quite convinced by my explanation that I had a brother who was three years old.

As I lay in my hospital bed, Matron arrived with a student nurse and instructed the girl to listen to the foetal hearts. The poor girl was nervous and was at first unable to locate them. 'Look,' said Matron impatiently. 'There's one head, and there's the other!'

When she had departed, I said to the junior nurse, 'Hugh's head was the other way up.'

That kind girl told me, 'Oh, sometimes they're one way up, sometimes another.'

She could easily have said 'They are both breeches', which was the case and would have terrified me, even though I would have had to ask her what it meant.

As it was, I spent an uncomfortable day being X-rayed from every possible angle knowing that Kenneth was going to induce the births the following day. Poor John and Daddy had to cope with the news that the twins were facing one another, and had not moved from that position since the first X-ray and 'might be joined'.

Fortunately, no one shared that information with me. Kenneth explained that some of his colleagues in the hospital were really interested in my twins and would like to watch their delivery. I assured him that I didn't mind if the entire audience of the Albert Hall wanted to watch it as long as we could get it over with. They were born on May 1st and I got rather tired of friends pointing out that it was Labour Day.

The delivery theatre was crowded, as Kenneth had

explained it would be. In those days it would have been very unusual for a father to be present at a hospital delivery, but John had been invited to witness Hugh's birth and was now invited to be there for the twins. He adamantly refused both times. He knew too much about obstetrics and what might go wrong to want to be there, which he felt might be a distraction for the consultant doing the job.

That was what he said, but I know he just couldn't face watching me in labour. I need not go into the details of the delivery but Maureen arrived first, followed eleven minutes later by Tommy, to be greeted by a big cheer from Kenneth's colleagues and someone shouting, 'Ladies first!' Maureen weighed in at six pounds six ounces, a good weight for a non-twin, but Tommy, at seven pounds nine ounces exceeded his older brother's weight.

John had been convinced from the outset that both would be boys, as there were so few girls in his family. When he arrived he neglected to say 'well done, darling' or something equally appropriate to me. His first words were 'Where's my daughter?'

I used to tell him that fate had definitely had the last laugh on him – the twins were followed by four more daughters. I had made up my mind that the baby girl would be called Catherine, after my beloved Granny, and wrote to tell her so. Back came an immediate reply, 'I have always hated the name. It seems to me that their names are quite obvious.' So Maureen and Tommy it was, and my parents were delighted.

The next baby we called Alice, John's mother's name. When I wrote to Granny about that, she wrote back and said, 'Maybe you'll call the next one after me.'

I was so upset. Her suggesting my parents' names for the twins was a typical act of generosity, but I had believed her when she told me she didn't like her own name. When Alice was succeeded by our fifth child, we called her Catherine. Sadly, Granny died when Catherine was three weeks old; John and Daddy decided that it would be inadvisable for me to go to her funeral as her namesake was so young. I was too used to doing what I was told, especially by Daddy, but I should have been there and always regret that I wasn't.

- CHAPTER NINE - READING FOR THE BAR

Once we had acquired the twins, the most important thing was to acclimatise Hugh, then aged twenty months, to the new additions to the family. John and I had given quite a lot of thought to this. When we believed I was expecting one baby, we introduced him to as many babies as possible, always encouraging him to admire them and wish that we too could have a baby in our family. We decided not to mention that there were going to be two.

When we brought them home, Hugh had not seen me for more than a month. I had been admitted to hospital a few days before they were born and at that time new mothers spent at least three weeks in hospital after a birth. My parents had kindly offered to look after him. He had settled in very happily, with Mike to play with.

We decided that we would leave the babies with Mrs Young, the practice housekeeper, when we went to Hornchurch to collect him. I was upset because initially it was quite clear that he had no idea who I was. Quite understandable, when you think that the last time he had seen me I had been so enormous. He was playing happily on the floor with Mike, smiled politely at me, and continued with their game.

Mummy and I were chatting and she said

something that made me laugh. Hugh stood up and came over to put his hands on my knee and look up into my face – he had recognised the sound of my voice and wanted a cuddle, even though my bulk was so completely different.

John and I had laid careful plans. We would take him home, give him his tea and his bath, and say nothing about the twins until the next morning. But fate had other ideas: one of the twins started to cry. Hugh headed for the stairs at once and came down joyfully, pointing upwards. 'Babies!' he proclaimed delightedly and conducted us upstairs to share *his* discovery. Quite honestly, I believe that it never crossed his mind that they would be any sort of competition for him – it might have been more problematic if there had only been one.

So we settled into our new routine, and we were so lucky to have dear Mrs Young. She came in every day, did the cleaning and most of the cooking. All I had to do was to care for the three children. As I mentioned, to get to our kitchen or out into the garden I had to cross the hall where the next two patients would be awaiting their turn. They all loved to get a glimpse of the twins. One remarked to her friend, 'Easy to see their Dad's in the business!'

But one morning I was astonished when John failed to get out of bed and asked if I would mind asking Seán to come up and have a look at him. It then turned out that he had a roaring appendix problem. Apparently he had known about it for weeks, but failed to mention because he thought I had enough on my plate.

It didn't take Seán long to diagnose the issue. He wanted to send for an ambulance but John categorically refused to allow the patients to see him carried off on a stretcher. So one of our friends took him to the hospital in his car. The surgeon telephoned and told me he would operate straight away. This was mid-morning.

Fortunately I had no knowledge of surgery, and when the day dragged on without any news from the hospital, I did not realise how serious that might be.

When Seán finished his evening consultations I was surprised and grateful when he said he would just stay with me until I had some news. We were in the kitchen and I was looking down at the floor. Even today when I close my eyes I can see the pattern on that linoleum.

At long last the phone rang. It was the surgeon. All he said was, 'I wouldn't like to have had to do that tomorrow.'

Two of my aunts came down to be with me; both were teachers and fortunately it was the summer holidays. When John was discharged from hospital it was obviously quite impossible that he should attempt to convalesce on the surgery premises. Our accountant recommended a pub situated just outside Hever Castle. Little as we could afford it, we had to accept that John needed to rest there.

We had a good friend called Michael Banahan – another doctor whom Daddy would describe as a 'typical Irish bachelor'. He was more than kind and offered to drive me down to see John for a few hours every afternoon. The aunties looked after the twins and Hugh came with us to see his Daddy. The publican kept a few chickens, and sitting outside in the garden I heard Hugh utter, 'Oh dear!' very disapprovingly, and realised that one of the chickens had done its business on the grass.

On the day before John was due to come home he phoned me. 'I have to go back into the hospital.'

Apparently the occurrence the surgeon had dreaded had taken place: there had been a perforation and repeat surgery would be necessary to save his life. Convalescence would have to be repeated. I would not like to have to re-live those weeks again. I was still breast feeding the twins; not only had the pub in Hever cost us more than we could afford, but John had also been compelled to employ a locum to take some of the burden from Seán.

But, thanks to God and to the help we had from family members and good friends, we survived it all somehow. John never had a day of illness again until his sudden death at the age of eighty. Life in our home resumed its routine. I really enjoyed being able to take the babies into John' s surgery between patients to say goodnight to Daddy, and having a cup of coffee with him after the surgery and before he left to do his daily home visits.

It was later that year that a friend phoned to tell me that she knew of an Italian *au pair* who was very unhappy in the family where she was living. They asked if I would be interested in taking her on.

'What would I do with an Italian *au pair*?' I asked John. Mrs Young and I operated as a great team, we didn't need anyone else.

'You could take your Bar finals,' he said.

And I could prove Daddy wrong again! In those days, as unbelievable as it seems now, you could actually take a correspondence course preparing you for the finals; the examinations themselves were held in London.

So dear Renata came to be part of our family and I embarked on the course. One essential component was that you had to take a timed test at home as the finals approached, to see whether the tutors on the course thought you were ready for them. Also I had to finish eating my dinners, which I did.

I tried to make time to watch Hugh's favourite children's programme on TV with him every day. As the pressure of study was building up, I experimented with switching it on and leaving him alone to enjoy it. That did not work at all – he followed me into the room where I was trying to study. 'It *is* called *Watch With Mother*,' he reminded me reproachfully.

All three children contracted measles just before the date of the test. Hugh, in particular, got the disease especially badly and had to be in a darkened room, which made study impossible even had I been capable of it with the children ill.

The only thing to do was to contact the college and postpone the timed test, maybe until the next session of examinations. I was quite surprised to find that there was a human being at the other end of the line, even more surprised to learn that he knew my name and had been supervising the work I had posted in. When I explained my predicament, he told me that he considered I was ready for the exams without doing the timed test. What a relief!

So I took the finals when the children had recovered and somehow or other managed to pass them. By the time I was called to the Bar we knew I was expecting

Alice, so I never had the slightest intention of practising.

Daddy was more than delighted to have been proved doubly wrong. I realise now that he had been administering a bit of psychology, knowing that it would spur me on to get my qualifications (which he would have described as 'a meal ticket') much more effectively than had he merely expressed a hope that I would finish my training. And it worked!

As soon as I had passed my exams I began to look for ways of helping with our income. The first pocket money I was able to earn was through my friend Neil. He needed my typing skills to present his business letters in the way the tuition at St James's had taught me to set them out. I think he actually lent me a typewriter. He paid me £2 a letter, which was very generous, and I usually had a few to type every week.

Jock was an old friend who worked in the children's department at Macmillan. He began to use my editing skills by sending me American children's books which I had to translate into English for the benefit of the English child reader. He would also send me proofs of other childrens' books for correction. I remember once posting a set of proofs back to him at the Bromley post office in the morning and hearing him congratulate me on the telephone because they had arrived at the office that afternoon. Such were the postal services we enjoyed in those days, with several collections and deliveries every day!

With the limited accommodation we had, it was fairly obvious that living on the surgery would have to come to an end now that I was expecting our fourth child. Not only that, John was getting embarrassed when the more outspoken patients began to ask him, 'Don't you know what's causing it, doctor?'

Seán kindly agreed that we could move to a larger house. He and John engaged a resident housekeeper to take over my duties. We found Larkfield, which was to be our family home for almost forty years. It was a large property on three floors with seven bedrooms, a butler's pantry and a maid's sitting room. Having no prospect of engaging either a butler or a maid, we quickly amalgamated the two small rooms to make a new and larger kitchen, with the help of Jim McNamara, a builder who sounded even more Irish than John. He and his wife Mary became lifelong friends of ours.

I was finding it difficult to understand what Jim said at first. When he left us after a discussion about the necessary work, I asked John what an 'Irish Jay' was and was told by my amused husband that Jim had been talking about an RSJ – a rolled steel joist. That didn't mean much to me either.

The old kitchen had been a gloomy place with a high window, giving scarcely any view of the lovely garden which we inherited. The couple who sold it to us had been given an acre of ground as a wedding present from her father who owned all the land around there. Larkfield was the first house to be built on what eventually became an unmade road in Bickley, situated between Bromley and Chislehurst. The road has remained unmade to this day and was a great place for the children to play with their friends without any risk of some car coming down at any speed.

The vendors kindly offered us their gardener. He

was earning £7 a week and, we were told, would even stoke the boiler as well! Needless to say we couldn't afford him. When we had been living there a few days John decided to tackle a bit of gardening. The gardener from next door put his head over the fence and asked, 'What are they like?'

'What are who like?'

'The new owners.'

John said, 'They're all right when you get used to them.'

The neighbouring house was called Ruffield and had been the second property built on what was to become a road called Hill Brow. Hugh was always a friendly child and set out to explore for any neighbouring children on our first day. He was soon back, looking a little downcast. 'Am I three 'n 'alf?' he enquired. I confirmed that he was. '*They're* four!' he explained. But there were several children of about his age living close to us and before long age ranking was forgotten and they were all playing together happily.

The occupants of Ruffield initially appeared to be rather a grand family and I was a bit scared of them. Shortly after Alice was born the following January I was bathing her on the counter in the kitchen when, to my horror, Hugh led Mrs Ross through the back door and announced that he had brought her to see 'our new baby'.

She explained that Hugh was already a great friend of her family because he had been in the habit of visiting them when they were having breakfast every morning. Their dining room had a low window and Hugh would lean on the sill to have a chat, knowing him probably having a snack too, but she was much too polite to mention that.

In fact she was charming and her equally charming husband became very fond of all our children. Mr Ross would find a sixpence in his pocket every time he came across Hugh or Tommy, which ensured his popularity with them. They had three grown-up children, but neither then nor later had any grandchildren of their own, which I think made them very sad.

Of course John and I could not possibly keep the garden or the grass tennis court up to the standard of people who had employed a full-time gardener, but John did his best, sporadically assisted by our friend Frank the tramp.

By the time Alice arrived we had acquired a second *au pair* girl, Luisa the sister of Renata. They were in quite different circumstances from normal *au pairs* because their mother was actually living and working in an Italian restaurant in London, so they had come not with the purpose of learning English, but just to be close to her.

Their father had been left behind in Italy. A girl from the same village was an *au pair* in a family living close to us. She told us that our girls' parents were known for their violent disagreements, throwing shoes and other objects that came to hand at one another, so that their neighbours took care to cross the road outside their home to avoid being hit by something flying out of a window. No wonder their poor mother had emigrated to London.

So when Luisa arrived, Renata gave up any attempt to speak English and Luisa didn't even bother to make a start. This resulted in my having to learn Italian, which had not been the object of the exercise. I could soon manage passably. John would come home and say it was like being in a foreign country as the three of us nattered on.

Interestingly, Hugh and the twins became bi-lingual in their early years. If we took them into an Italian shop or restaurant in Soho, the staff would surround them with cries of delight and give them far too many sweets and pastries as soon as they recognised that they could speak and understand in their own language.

In my case, my newly acquired linguistic proficiency led to a rather embarrassing incident. Some friends had an Italian lady visiting and invited me to be her partner in a bridge game. At one point I looked at my hand and came out with an expression frequently heard at home, which I had supposed to be the equivalent of 'oh dear'.

Truly scandalised, my partner laid her cards on the table and enquired in a faint voice where I had come across this expression, which I will not repeat here for fear that one of my readers might understand the language.

The mother of the girls would come down for the weekend sometimes, offering to cook for us in return for our hospitality. She would produce vast amounts of her delicious pasta recipes, far too much for us to make more than a dent in the quantities heaped on our plates in such profusion, and then become almost tearful because our appetites were not up to them.

During one such weekend John and I returned late

after having been guests at a dinner party at a friend's house. Mother and daughters had already gone to bed and John had forgotten his keys. We rang the doorbell several times, thumped on the door knocker more times, threw stones up at their bedroom windows, but there was no response. The only downstairs window that was open was a very small one next to the little cloakroom.

When it was clear that the three visitors must have been dead to the world, John decided that there was nothing for it but for him to attempt to squeeze through the tiny window. He was a big man, still seventeen and a half stone, with the height to go with it. Unfortunately he was wearing his one decent suit; the only way to avoid damaging it was to take it off!

He stripped to his underwear, handed me the garments and managed somehow to wriggle through. All I could think about was the possibility that our new neighbours were able to witness this unusual scene. If they did they were far too well mannered to refer to it.

Next morning, however, the signora and her two daughters were anxious to tell us about the terrible night they had experienced – woken up by people ringing bells, banging, and even throwing stones at their windows. They were proud to tell us that they had sensibly put their heads under their pillows and ignored it all!

- CHAPTER TEN - MORE BABIES

After settling into Larkfield, we continued the policy of having two *au pair* girls at a time, plus a daily cleaner. John believed that mothers of several children become exhausted, not from giving birth, but from the amount of work the family inevitably generates. We did not again make the mistake of having two of the same nationality together because most *au pairs* come to learn English, so it would have been unfair.

The twins, instead of being more work than one baby, were so absorbed in one another that all they needed from us was regular amounts of food and care. They were able to communicate in their own language. Maureen, always ahead of Tommy at that stage, learned to speak first and would translate Tommy's needs and requirements to us.

At primary school she continued to play this role. When the headmistress, Miss Preedy, pointed out to Tom that a page in his exercise book was rather untidy, his response was, 'But look at Maureen's!' He just considered his twin to be an extension of himself.

When they were about three, Tommy had to be admitted to hospital for a few days for minor surgery. Maureen was completely distraught and inconsolable. We had owned a puppy which unfortunately died, so we had told the children that Blackie had gone for a little holiday.

When we made the mistake of explaining that Tommy had gone for a little holiday, Hugh started to cry. 'I don't want Tommy going for a little holiday like Blackie and never coming back!'

It was at that point that we decided that there was going to be a boys' bedroom and a girls' bedroom. We could foresee great difficulties in trying to separate the twins if we left it any later.

For my last four pregnancies I always secretly hoped it might be twins again. You would certainly never have the problem of a bored baby.

Maureen was always the 'head girl' in the family, never afraid to speak her mind. One Christmas we had a visit from two priest friends. They admired the crib we always set up in the sitting room and one of them decided to test Maureen's familiarity with the story.

'Who's that?'

'That's Our Lady.'

'And who's that?'

'That's Saint Joseph.'

'And who's this?'

'*That's* Baby Jesus,' she said, losing her patience, 'but *you* should know all this already!'

Tommy was quieter than Maureen and quite a thinker. In the bath one day he asked, 'Why did God invent sweets when they are bad for your teeth?'

Interestingly, he became a dentist.

He and Maureen remained particularly close even in adulthood. When Tom acquired his first home, he invited all the family to dinner there. When Maureen arrived first, she was told that he was just going to have a shower. 'Steaks are in the fridge, salads need to be made, table needs to be set,' he informed her, taking it for granted he could leave all the preparations to her in his absence. Every 1st May they would take a day's holiday, meet up for lunch, choose birthday presents for one another and finish their day meeting up with all the family for dinner. They both married in the same year. Maureen's husband was Australian so they have lived on opposite sides of the world ever since.

The children's eyesight was being checked at primary school. We had an urgent message that Hugh's sight was so bad that we needed to make an appointment with an eye specialist. John immediately found a consultant at Guy's Hospital. He had a number of medical students around him when the consultant rather unkindly announced that, because Hugh's father was a GP, he had illogically been diagnosed with a problem when his eyesight was actually perfect.

What had not occurred to us was that either the school or the oculist had mixed up the boys' names, so it was not until a couple of years later that poor Tom was diagnosed with severe sight problems. John was not going to repeat his Guy's experience, so he took Tom to a local optician who immediately recommended that he see a consultant. Not the same one!

I was making marmalade on the January day when Alice Jane decided to put in her appearance. John came home for his lunch as usual and I told him that I thought I was having contractions. He wanted to check and took me upstairs, followed as usual by Hugh. Once I had got myself on to the bed, John put his hand on my tummy glancing at his watch to check the frequency of the contractions. Hugh put his hand beside John's and glanced at an imaginary watch on his own wrist.

At four years old Hugh was convinced that the words 'man' and 'doctor' were interchangeable. We had discovered this when he opened the door to a delivery man and came to announce that there was a 'doctor' at the door. This, I suppose, was unsurprising in that every male he knew happened to be a doctor: his grandfather, John, Seán, Frank, his Uncle John, together with our many friends in the profession. So on that cold winter day Hugh was sure that he was doing exactly whatever Daddy was doing.

I went downstairs to check on my marmalade – you have to put a little of the mix into the fridge on a saucer to test whether it will set, taking it out after a few minutes to see whether it is ready to be put into the waiting sterilised jars. I asked John to help with that, but we got into a great deal of confusion because every time I said, 'Now' poor John would ask, 'Marmalade or contraction?'

Marmalade safely in jars, he decided that he should take me to the hospital without delay and returned to his evening surgery. Alice arrived within a couple of hours and was by far the easiest delivery I had, although at ten and a half pounds by far the largest. As it happened, one of the junior doctors in the hospital was the husband of a friend of mine from King's. When

John, summoned by the telephone, arrived outside the labour ward, he asked an emerging midwife if the baby was a boy or a girl. 'Can't stop now,' she explained, hurrying past him, 'I have to tell Doctor Garson first!'

Not surprisingly, when Alice was a little girl we often sang the ditty *'They're Changing Guard at Buckingham Palace,* Christopher Robin went down with Alice...'

She opened the back door to an astonished milkman one day, when she was little and introduced herself: 'Hello, I'm Alice – *Buckingham* Alice.'

Alice was considerate as a child. When she was six they were all posting letters to Father Christmas; hers said, 'I want to be sensible this year. I would like an umbrella.'

She was a very keen ballet dancer and got good grades in several of the Royal Ballet School examinations. The last one she took was at a time when she was ill. The examiner said to her teacher, 'When that child danced, my heart moved.'

Eighteen months after Alice, Catherine arrived, named after my beloved Granny who was always known as Kate. When she was little she was usually known as Cathy and told me, 'You only call me Catherine when you're cross with me, Mummy.' Since growing up she has chosen to be called Katie. That might have something to do with the fact that her song was *'K-K-K-Katie'*.

Always a mischievous child, she disappeared one day when she could barely walk. The other children, the *au pairs* and I searched the house, searched the garden, searched the street with mounting panic. No sign of her. We called and called her name, but there was not a sound. John was over at the surgery.

In the end I phoned the police. Not very reassuringly, the first question they asked was whether we had a pond anywhere near us. Luckily we did not. Two officers turned up in a patrol car. By that time our dear friend Dick Buckley, whose dental practice was much closer than John's, had abandoned his patients to come to help.

We were all standing in the front garden discussing what the next step should be when we heard a little giggle coming from an outhouse where the rubbish bins were stored. My naughty daughter had managed to hide herself in there and close the door. She had enjoyed listening to all the searches and the calls, but now she was ready to come out.

Her best friend at primary school was Nuala Buckley. 'I've got the same dress as Nuala Buckley,' she informed me with satisfaction one day. 'I've got the same socks and shoes as Nuala Buckley *and* I've got the same blazer as Nuala Buckley ... Someone might see me walking along the road and say to themselves, '*There's* Nuala Buckley!'

That's devotion for you!

Nora was born next. She was three years old when Mary Rose, our seventh, joined us, and very much appreciating her status as baby to the family. When John and I told the children that Mary Rose was on the way she asked, 'What means it – a *new* baby?'

John and I did our best to explain. Her brothers and sisters had all been there before and were looking forward to the addition to the family. Mary was born a month before Hugh's tenth birthday, so we had seven children under ten and each one was welcomed; we both loved children.

But poor Nora was not so sure. The night I arrived home from the hospital, she came into the bedroom where I was feeding the baby, carrying her toy suitcase and with her teddy under her arm. 'I've come to say goodbye,' she told me. 'I'm going to live with the Fletts across the road. They haven't got a baby and you don't need me anymore!'

Somehow I managed to convince her that indeed we did need her, and we couldn't possibly do without her.

In the end she relented and agreed to stay, but it was touch and go. As the youngest two, she and Mary Rose became very close as they grew up and are very close to this day. One thing that certainly helped is that Nora was allowed to choose the baby's name – her best friend's name was Mary, so that was the deciding factor.

Nora was an artistic child, loved flowers and pretty clothes. One day in spring Hugh came home from school to discover Nora, aged four, happily humming to herself while carefully detaching each head from a neighbour's display of daffodils along the bed fronting their garden on Hill Brow. John and I had to make our apologies and offer a bottle of wine in restitution.

Almost as soon as she could walk she would go to the chest of drawers holding the girls' clothes and rummage until she found a pretty petticoat or some other item which took her fancy, then demand to be dressed in it. One Christmas, when she was about five, she offered to deliver the cards addressed to our neighbours along the road. She was back with lightning speed. 'Did you deliver them all?' I asked incredulously.

'A lucky thing happened,' she told me. 'I met the postman and I gave them to him!'

Nora never liked to admit that she didn't understand some words that were new to her. One cold night I was tucking her into bed and asked her, 'Would you like a duvet?'

'Have you got a banana?' she asked cautiously.

During the months before Mary Rose was born I had found myself worrying, for the first time in a pregnancy. I sensed that John felt the same although we never discussed it. We had been so extremely fortunate to be blessed with six healthy children, were we pushing our luck?

When another perfect baby arrived we felt that it was time to call a halt.

My parents had, frankly, greeted announcement of the last three expected with distinctly progressive lack of enthusiasm. But when the children were actually there they were welcomed and became a source of pride. They were amazing grandparents, generous and much loved. In his news book at school Hugh wrote, 'Christmas begins when Granny and Grandpa arrive at our house!'

Of course, we had to take our turn with the Keefes, but wherever the grandparents and Mike were for the festive season we would all get together for Boxing Day, traipsing through the Blackwall Tunnel in one direction or the other. Jimmy and Biddy would join us with their four children too.

Mary, in contrast to Nora, did not enjoy her position

as the youngest member of the tribe. The children often played croquet on what had been the tennis court. Mary was perpetually asking, 'Is it my turn yet?' and it never seemed to be. She used to say that she was convinced there was a secret hiding place somewhere in the house where all her brothers and sisters would conceal themselves from her.

Even when she had started school, she could be heard asking plaintively, 'Why is it that nobody in this family seems to realise that there are question marks at the end of my questions?'

The trouble was, of course, that everyone would be talking at once. When Mary got to university she joined the debating club. 'Where did you learn to debate like that?' the lecturer running the club asked.

'Round the kitchen table,' was the reply.

Mary Rose has always been a strong character. She and John had their battles, especially at meal times. My rule was always, 'You don't have to eat anything you don't like, but if you ask for something you have to eat it.'

Mary didn't pay a lot of attention to that and would often decide to leave most of her meal on her plate. John would tell her to eat up, she would close her mouth mutinously, eventually sliding down from her chair, crawling under the table and exiting the room. John would forbid me to go after her but, of course, I would go and persuade her to come and back and say 'sorry'.

We did not believe in physical punishment but, when correction was unavoidable, would direct the offender to sit on the bottom step of the staircase and think about things until they were ready to make amends. I have to confess, however, that there were occasions when some misbehaviour drove me to the point of giving one of them a – gentle – smack. They laugh now and remind me that I would then burst into tears and say, 'Now look what you've made me do!'

They all remember the famous occasion when I had baked a cake and someone had taken a slice before I had given permission. I lined them up and asked the culprit to confess. No one would admit to it. I think it was the only time I ever said, 'Wait till your daddy gets home!'

So they knew they were in big trouble, not that John would have done anything to punish them, which they also knew. But I was really cross because one of them was lying to me and that was unusual enough for me to make the empty threat.

So when John did come home from the surgery I told him what had happened. The culprit owned up immediately. 'It was me,' he admitted.

- CHAPTER ELEVEN -
BIG HUGH

One very important member of our family has not been mentioned yet. One of John's older brothers, Hugh, had tragically lost his young wife to cancer some years earlier, leaving his brother to care for two young sons, the eldest also named Hugh, not after his father but for his grandfather as was the Irish family tradition.

Hugh remarried; very sadly his new wife did not get on with his eldest son. Young Hugh, who was five when he lost his mother, could remember her and that might have been one cause of the difficulties; whatever it was, his father wrote to John to tell him that Hugh was coming to England to enlist as an apprentice in the Royal Air Force.

John and I discussed this, and John immediately wrote back to his brother to say that we would be happy to have Hugh, then sixteen years old, living with us so that he could pass the ordinary school exams and enter the RAF as an officer cadet.

His father did not reply to that letter. A couple of weeks later we had a telephone call from young Hugh to explain that he had started his apprenticeship and he asked, very shyly, if it would be all right for him to come and see us on his first leave. From the moment he came through the door, he just became our eldest son.

Our Hugh was ten months old, sitting in his high chair, and I can remember the first thing his cousin did was remove his uniform cap and put it on baby Hugh's head to make us all laugh.

The difficulty about names was easily solved – he became 'Big Hugh' to family and friends from that time on. Very sadly, the problems with his own family remained. By the time he came to us there were several little stepbrothers and sisters at home in Ireland; for his first Christmas away Big Hugh spent the little money he had on presents for all of them, and presents for us too.

His stepmother repacked his parcel and posted it back to him. He was always so fond of our children that I can only guess how it must have hurt. He was absent from our home on duty a good deal of the time, but whenever he had any leave he would be on the doorstep.

As my children grew up, he would pitch in and help with whatever was going on, peeling vegetables for meals, feeding the odd baby cousin, taking the older ones out for walks.

When Alice was born he became her godfather.

Every Christmas Big Hugh would take all the children out for some treat on Christmas Eve, to give me a chance to get on with the preparations undistracted. He always made a great fuss of Alice, his godchild. This meant a good deal to Alice: when you are the middle child in a family of seven, having someone with a special interest in you is incredibly important. But all the children adored him. He always called me 'Dear'.

Hugh did very well in his career in the RAF and was eventually recommended for promotion to become an officer. There was a snag – the minimum qualification required was an O-level in English. Hugh studied for that in his spare time and acquired it without too much difficulty. After that there were months of interviews and medical checks. At last, he rang me from Germany where he was stationed at the time, 'Only one more medical, Dear. I'm coming over to London for it, so see you soon.'

Heartbreakingly, he did not pass that last medical. He had been born with a disability called ankylosing spondylitis, an arthritic spinal condition which appears in teenagers or adults, develops over a lifetime, and can cause severe pain in the back, rib cage and neck. Eventually it can result in curvature of the spine, causing the victim to bend forward permanently. I had no idea that Hugh suffered from this condition or indeed was experiencing any pain from it. If he were, it was John he would have told. I don't know that John was even aware of the problem.

What was so cruel was that the disability had been detected when Hugh first joined the RAF. Had those who put him through the other medical tests and allowed him to hope bothered to look at his medical records, they could have told him at that stage that there was no chance of his being accepted for officer training.

He was devastated and not surprisingly. By that time he was well qualified in technology; he left the RAF and obtained a good job some distance away from us. But bad fortune had not finished with him yet.

At the time, staff at all the Irish banks were on a long strike. Hugh's father was a bank clerk and there were six children from his second marriage to support. Like many of his colleagues, he came over to England to try to find a job and send money home. The only work available for him was as a labourer. He took digs in London and would come down to Bickley every weekend.

Big Hugh was delighted to meet up with his father after so many years and they very soon established a close and loving relationship. John too was so happy to be with his brother again. For a few short months we all enjoyed those weekends together.

It was then that disaster struck. Hugh's father had a massive heart attack in the digs. He survived for two days in hospital, where we could have visited him. His landlady told the police that he had a brother who was a doctor in Bickley. Unbelievably, the police could not locate John because, they said, his practice was in Welling. We were in the telephone directory, but apparently it had not occurred to the police force to check that.

The terrible result was that Hugh's father died alone in the London hospital. That was such a shattering blow for poor Big Hugh and John. Having so recently had to cope with his disappointment about the RAF, which his father was helping him to overcome, Big Hugh was struggling alone to bear a burden which was about to overwhelm him, coupled, very possibly, with an amount of physical pain which he knew could only increase as he grew older.

Then came the day when I took the telephone call

from a police officer who wanted to speak to John, not a sufficiently unusual event to cause me any alarm – John on several occasions had been sought out by police officers investigating some matter relating to one of his patients. The officer left his own number and asked that John call him as soon as he came home – an act of compassion for me, to ensure that I would not be alone when I heard the purpose of the call. Which was to tell us that Big Hugh had taken his own life, at the age of twenty-seven.

John was escorted in a police car to identify him, my brother Jimmy cancelled his afternoon dental surgery to go with him. The pain and grief were indescribable. I simply could not understand that my adopted son had not left a message for me. I searched all over his room for a message and continued to believe that I would find it one day – certainly for years.

Poor John blamed himself for not diagnosing that Hugh was schizophrenic. He believed that his mental illness stemmed back to the loss of his mother when he was five, told me that Hugh had been unbelievably calm about it at the time which, in the light of hindsight, suggested that the child blamed himself for his loss, rationalising that it was his 'naughtiness' which had been the cause of it.

John explained to me that his illness made him compartmentalise his life, that because the tragedy took place in the area where he worked, Hugh, in his disordered state of mind, would have thought that we would never know anything about it. Not being medical myself, I have no idea whether this ties in with psychiatric thinking or whether John just made it up to try to console me.

As soon as he heard what had happened, dear Canon Joe, one of our closest friends, turned up on the doorstep. 'Maureen,' he said, 'You've got to get John through this.'

It occurs to me that he would have given John exactly the same message about me. Something I have noticed is that the tragedy of losing a child either brings the parents closer together or drives them apart. One barrister friend of mine was rushing to get to court one day and catastrophically reversed his car out of the garage without realising that his two-year-old son had somehow managed to get behind it. Very sadly, he and his wife blamed one another – she because she could not believe that he had not seen the child, he because he could not believe that she had not been careful enough to keep him out of the way. Eventually it was the end of their marriage. Another couple we knew had a twelve-year-old daughter who died in a riding accident. Their marriage suffered a similar fate.

John and I were much more fortunate. Somehow what had happened drew us closer together. Each of us blamed ourselves, he because he missed the schizophrenia, me because I knew that I had so much less time to give to Big Hugh now that there were seven younger ones in the house. Shortly before it happened, he had said to me one day, 'We never seem to have time to talk any more, dear.'

How often have I wondered if that were a cry for help which I was too busy to answer.

The major problem was to try to keep what had happened from the children – they were devastated enough to learn that they would never see him again, their adored older brother. Hugh, our eldest, was twelve years old. We told them that Big Hugh had died in an accident and they assumed that it was a car accident. Now of course they all know the truth, but it is only very recently that I have been able to talk to them about it.

In her early twenties, Alice married Pat, who always claims to be my 'numero uno' son-in-law because he was the first. They have two grown-up sons.

When Alice was expecting her first son, he delayed his arrival for more than a fortnight.

Nowadays the birth would be induced but at that time medical intervention was not popular. On the Sunday before he was born, John and I were at Mass and I suddenly 'knew' that the baby would be a boy and that he would be born on the twentieth anniversary of Big Hugh's death, a few days later. He did arrive on that anniversary and was baptised with three Christian names: 'John' for my husband, 'James' for his other grandfather, and 'Hugh'.

I had always wanted to write. Apart from the CTS pamphlets on marriage, my first ventures into print included a job with our local newspaper. Businesses in the area would purchase a whole page to advertise their wares. My task would be to compose about 1500 words of deathless prose, praising the products of the advertiser and destined to appear in the middle of the page surrounded by the adverts, in the hope of attracting the interest of our readers.

Naturally, there were a great variety of topics. I

remember once complaining to the editor, when a garden centre had booked the page, that I knew nothing about growing flowers, fruit or vegetables.

'Come on, Maureen,' he said encouragingly. 'What did you know about plumbing last week?'

Unanswerable in the circumstances.

Much later, when I had joined chambers, a couple of the members were earning themselves an extra crust in the evenings by vetting next day's newspapers for potentially libellous comments before they were published. In those days all the main publications had huge offices in Fleet Street, just across the road from us.

I never went in for that because, of course, I had to get back to my husband and children. But one of my friends asked me, as a great favour, to stand in for him one night. It was a complete revelation to me – so busy, everyone rushing around and shouting, waving pieces of paper, all in a terrible state of excitement.

I was very impressed because one of the journalists working near me was Bernard Levin. I recognised him from the TV, and I enjoyed reading his regular column in *The Times*. He identified me as a complete novice and decided to amuse himself by embarrassing me, shouting round the room to each of his colleagues in turn asking whether anyone had seen his missing 'French letter'.

But his joke misfired: never having heard the expression, I concluded that he really had mislaid a letter in the French language and could not understand the amusement of his fellow journalists until I got back to chambers and asked the others about it.

- CHAPTER TWELVE -
FAMILY LIFE

Having achieved my call to the Bar, I had put the law behind me, as far as I knew. For the next sixteen years I thoroughly enjoyed bringing up the children, making lasting friendships with a number of like-minded couples with families of our children's ages, learning to play golf rather badly, and starting a career as a freelance writer in my spare time.

We had a series of lovely *au pair* girls to help with the children; as John commented any girl who came to a family of our size was likely to be a nice person. I have contact with some of them in Barcelona to this day. We had some from Holland, one from the German countryside and one from France, always two at a time in the busy years.

When Nora was about to be born, Teresa's mother died suddenly in Spain, and of course she had to return for the funeral. Hilda from Germany needed a partner urgently to help her cope until I came home from hospital, which in those days was three weeks after the birth. Our house had become an informal club for the Spanish *au pairs* in the locality so I appealed to them desperately. Did anyone know a girl who would like to come?'

'Well,' said one, after a great deal of thought, 'my

aunt would *love* to come!'

Then she laughed and added, 'But she's old enough to be your mother!'

That didn't matter to me at all. Dear Tia Amparo arrived in the nick of time and mothered not only the children but also poor Hilda, who had a rather unhappy home life back in Germany. She stayed for six months and lived to be a hundred. I was invited to the celebration a couple of years ago but was too ancient myself to accept the invitation.

The father of one of the Dutch girls was a newspaper editor. Thea had come to us for three weeks and stayed for eighteen months. When she was about to go home I asked her to put an advertisement for a replacement in her father's newspaper. 'Of course,' she smiled. 'I will put "very nice family – special the husband"!'

She may have been the one who told me, after she had been with us for months, that she had always believed that John's Christian name was 'Honestly John' which turned out to be an expression which I, unknowingly, was in the habit of using when I talked to him.

We loved all our girls and they became a valued part of the family during their time with us. Thea brought her boyfriend Ton to be vetted by us before she agreed to marry him. Naturally, we had a special dinner, with wines to accompany the courses. Afterwards, John produced liqueurs as was very much the fashion in those days. 'Oh-oh,' complained Thea, 'the glasses are getting smaller!'

John and I were invited to the wedding and placed

at the top table with Thea and Ton and their parents. In his speech Thea's father explained that we were her English parents. We were in touch for many years, with Thea coming to visit us sometimes as have some of the Spanish girls. Sadly I have not heard from her for a couple of Christmases now, and have no means of finding out what has happened.

From an early age, Tommy was in the habit of falling in love with the *au pairs* and promising to marry them when he grew up. In fact, we only stopped inviting them when the last very attractive young lady joined us when Hugh was about eighteen. He spent so much time taking her out with his friends in the evenings that she was far too tired to be a lot of use the following day.

Some were more useful than others of course. My parents had a cottage in Brightlingsea. I took the children there for a holiday plus the current *au pair* and an extra child, Maureen's friend, Christine Buckley. John came down for the weekend. I had taken the minibus and John was to drive my small car. Most unusually for him, he arrived very cross.

'The wretched key you left wouldn't start the car. I had to walk to a garage and get a new one,' he accused, handing me the offending object.

'Well, it starts it for me,' I replied, stuck it in the ignition and got the engine running immediately.

He was so angry that he said nothing, just took the car down to the town jetty and threw the offending artefact as far as he could out into the creek. That done, he resumed his normal happy disposition and we all had an enjoyable weekend. The key was never mentioned again.

Brightlingsea, a little village at the time, was a very popular destination for the children. The beaches tended to be stony, but who cares about that when you're young? A great friend for the whole family, from my parents downwards, was Old Jack, one of the locals who did a bit of gardening and various odd jobs for us, including keeping an eye on the place when we were not there.

He had already made up the beds and purchased bread, milk, tea and eggs, which were waiting for us on the kitchen table. Within a few minutes of our arrival he knocked on the front door, accepted a cup of tea and offered to do any other little errands which might help me. Seeing me surrounded by the eight children, all demanding to know when we could go down to Grandpa's beach hut and have a swim, he offered me little sympathy with his gloomy prediction, 'Oh, they're a headache when they're little, missus, but they're a heartache when they're grown.'

Hugh and Tommy, his special companions, trailed after him around the village constantly, fascinated by the tales he told them about his own boyhood. He must have been in his eighties, but never tired of recounting his adventures as a sailor when he had been young.

Sadly, it was only a short time after that holiday that we heard of Old Jack's death. Tommy, in particular, was inconsolable. 'Why did we not have a chance to say goodbye, Mummy?' he asked with a sob.

I tried to comfort him with the promise that, one day, he would see Old Jack in heaven. 'In fact, when you get to heaven the first person you'll see is Old Jack.'

This led to fresh tears. 'I don't want the first person I see to be Old Jack. I want it to be *you,* Mummy.'

The weather had been beautiful and we spent every day in Daddy's hut overlooking the beach, the pride and joy of his life at the time, furnished like a little palace, with a small cooker on which I could produce meals. Each spring Daddy was to be found giving it a new coat of paint, never happier than when one or more of his eighteen grandchildren was there to share the painting with him.

However, I had left John on his own and I realised how lonely he must be. I was missing him too. Apart from times when one of us had been hospitalised, one ill-fated bachelor golfing weekend with some of his hard drinking Irish friends, and one night I spent at my old convent boarding school, we were never separated for a night during the forty-seven years of our marriage.

The *au pair* and I packed the minibus with our belongings and the eight children, plus a huge bunch of Old Jack's home grown rhubarb – no seat belts in those days, when I think about it now it seems impossible. The journey would take at least two and a half hours, depending on traffic.

We were heading for the Blackwall Tunnel to take us back to Kent. Just as we came into Stratford, the point where traffic was at its heaviest, there was a scream from the *au pair.* One of the children had been sick over the rhubarb. What should she do?

I was giving her instructions over my shoulder when it struck me that all the traffic around us seemed to have disappeared. My minibus was the only moving vehicle.

I saw the enormous policeman in front of me just in time to brake. He walked slowly round to my window and said, 'Madam, I am not standing here just doing physical jerks.'

No indeed, he had been directing the traffic.

There was a wail from one of the children, 'Mummy, are we all going to prison?'

The officer put his head inside the window and inspected the interior.

'Oh, go on then,' he waved me ahead resignedly.

That was the first, last and only time I drove the family to Brightlingsea without John.

We were not well off financially. John got into the habit of going to a local street market first thing on market day with the objective of buying cheap tinned food and other supplies from one of the traders there.

If something was on special offer John would say, 'I'll take a case of that.'

After a few weeks of this, the market stallholder asked, 'Have you got a boarding house, mate?'

'No, just seven children.'

From then onwards, apparently deeply impressed, the salesman made a special point of letting John know the details of his best offers for that week as soon as he caught sight of him. One week it was loo rolls – fortunately we had a lot of attic space, so John returned with a car load.

Another week, never to be forgotten, it was prunes. By that time I was an inventive cook, nevertheless it got to the point where the children would ask suspiciously, 'Are there prunes in this, Mummy?'

But then John's friend introduced him to an even

better, and probably illegal, bargain. He would produce a case or two packed to the brim with tins which had lost their labels, for the sum of ten shillings (50p nowadays). They were undamaged tins of course, but you would have no idea of their contents until you opened one.

We soon discovered that all tinned food has a code or number punched into the tin itself, so the first thing was to sort the tins by their numbers. We then opened one of each kind, and labelled the remainder with the contents. The children found this tremendously exciting, as indeed it could be. Items like tinned figs or vine leaves, which it would never have occurred to me to purchase in the shops, turned out to be quite delicious.

Then came the day when John's friend really let us down. He had some plastic bags full of a white powder and marked 'MP', which he told John stood for milk powder. Naturally, John purchased some of the bags. He could count on me to find a use for dried milk.

And I did - I made ice cream with it. The children all loved ice cream but when it was served up to them for tea their spoons went down into their dishes, one by one.

'What's the matter?' I asked.

'Mummy, it tastes like something but I don't think it's ice cream,' Hugh told me.

I grabbed a spoon and tasted it myself. 'MP' stood, not for milk powder, but for mashed potato!

John's liking for a bargain, ably supported by mine I must confess, lasted into the children's teens when I had started to practise at the Bar. We were going out to celebrate someone's birthday at a local restaurant on one occasion. The local paper had an advertisement for our favoured eating house, offering a free bottle of wine for two people booking a table.

Off to court in the morning, when John was dropping me off at the station, we decided that he should purchase several additional copies of the paper to provide us with enough free wine for the whole family and probably some guests as well.

When he picked me up that evening the first thing I asked about was whether he had remembered to collect the necessary coupons. Something about the way he confirmed that he had them made me question it.

'You did buy the other copies of the paper?'

'Well – no. I just went into the public library and cut them out!'

I was aghast. 'John, if this gets out I could be disbarred and you could probably be struck off.'

He just found it funny.

John was in no sense a mean man. He was more than generous in most respects. But he did like a bargain. And we certainly needed them when the children were young.

One of the first foreign holidays we had was when we had just lost Big Hugh and the family of one of our Spanish girls generously invited us to stay in their seaside property; to get there we decided to take the car on the Portsmouth to Bilbao ferry and travel across Spain to our destination. As with all our holidays, Anne and Sarah Toal, together with my brother Mike made the party up to twelve. Fortunately the villa was spacious enough to accommodate everyone.

There were half-price fares for the children; a child under three years old went free. Mary Rose was under three when John booked but had celebrated her third birthday a few days before we sailed. Nothing could persuade her to separate herself from a birthday card badge pinned on her dress which proclaimed, 'Now I am Three.'

If any of the crew noticed it they said nothing.

The older children could all swim. I had worn a track between home and the local baths several times a week to get them all lessons. Maureen and Alice decided to raise a collection of pesetas from the eldest six siblings and Sarah to be called 'the rubber ring for Mary fund' and the ring was duly purchased so that Mary could follow them all into the sea.

Our host had kindly booked us into a rather luxurious hotel halfway across Spain.

To our embarrassment the hotel concierge emerged with a team of bell boys ready to carry our luggage to the bedrooms. Hugh and Tommy had never seen anything like the room they were to occupy. When they discovered a little bell push, which summoned one of the staff, they had great fun until we found out what they were doing.

We were all tired and hungry so descended to the restaurant as soon as we could. It was about nine in the evening; the *maitre' d* informed us that they did not start serving dinner until 10.30pm. John, Anne and I ordered some wine and some soft drinks for the children in the hope that the staff might relent and allow us to order earlier. They did neither.

Mary Rose decided to go in for some furniture removing and began to drag two of the chairs over the carpet. When asked what she was doing she replied, 'I just making a little bed for myself.'

The others were falling asleep with their heads on the tablecloth. But when the meal did come at last it was delicious. The weather was hot and our minibus was right hand drive; weighed down as it was by twelve passengers and their luggage, it was ponderously slow with virtually no acceleration.

Seated beside John, it was my duty to look ahead to see whether we needed to pass one of the huge, even more ponderous, lorries on the road, and if so where it would be safe to pull out and try to do it. I was totally exhausted by the time we arrived in the tiny village where we were to stay, but that was nothing to John's exhaustion. He was gasping for a beer.

In the small local bar I tried to order one for him. My Spanish was fairly adequate, but the kind nun who had been my teacher had certainly never thought it necessary to include the word 'beer' in her syllabus. The barman hopefully produced the French *aperitif* Byrrh which was definitely not what John had in mind.

Eventually the barman got the message and exclaimed '*cervezas*!' – a word I was never likely to forget in all our subsequent visits to Spain. I looked at John and asked Anne if it was the lighting that was making his face look yellow. Not at all, it was pure fatigue.

John was never a linguist, although he was taught the Irish language at school. The authorities were so keen to promote it that if you took any public exam – even maths! – in Irish, you got an extra ten per cent!

On one holiday we were driving across France, with our usual carload of twelve, when we needed to stop to get some additional cash. I can get by in French, so John parked the car outside a bank in a busy street and I went inside.

When I came out the children were wild with excitement. 'Daddy spoke French!'

This seemed unlikely so I asked what he had said.

A policeman came up waving his arms because we shouldn't be parked here and Daddy said, '*Oon momento*!'

– CHAPTER THIRTEEN – SCOOPING THE WORLD ON MARGARET THATCHER

John and I had busy and happy lives bringing up the children, playing bridge and golf with our friends (when we had the time), giving and going to dinner parties, a popular activity in those days. I had really learned to love cooking and was the first hostess in our crowd to introduce two exotic items to our friends.

Avocado pears were a delicacy much appreciated by Mummy and Daddy and were at that time being offered for sale by the more adventurous greengrocers. In Nigeria they had been growing them in their own garden they told us, and would just pluck two for breakfast.

The other, also inherited from Mummy, was garlic bread. After the dinner party when that was on my menu for the first time, one of my friends rang, sounding very cross. 'I've been to every bread shop in the area, and none of them have ever heard of garlic bread!'

Well, in those days you made your own – and how much better it tasted than what you can easily buy today.

The children's primary school was a short walk away, attached to the local Catholic church. Each child was given a 'My News' book where they would give an account of items of interest in their lives. Data protection had not been invented then. How I came to dread the revelations on those pages, which would be open for all to read on the children's desks at parents' evenings.

'When Mummy and Daddy have a dinner party we get the leftovers.'

'My mummy and daddy are not at all shy. My mummy has seven children.'

'Mummy and Daddy are never cross with us, unless we have been naughty or they are tired.'

'It is St Patrick's Day tomorrow and my mummy and daddy are going up to London to get married.' (This at the point where we already had five children!)

We were going to the annual Irish University ball and I had hung my ball dress and John's black tie suit and dress shirt in the spare room in readiness. Miss Preedy commented, 'I'm so glad he's going to make an honest woman of you at last!'

The most potentially dangerous 'news item' was posted by Mary Rose: 'My daddy goes to the IRA three times every week.'

In order to earn a bit more money John had an appointment as a medical examiner for new recruits at the RAF station at Biggin Hill, where he went for three weekly sessions held very early in the morning to accommodate his practice timetable. Mary was too young to know one set of initials from another; the IRA were active terrorists in Britain at the time and mention of them was constantly being made in the media. We were all too aware that John's Irish background would mean that he was being monitored by security services, as were all Irishmen living here then. Fortunately he wasn't arrested.

We played bridge regularly with the same couples; our system was that we had a kitty for each four players. Each couple put a pound in the kitty and the losers that evening put in a shilling for each hundred points they were down. When there was enough money in a kitty the four went out to dinner together. A great system.

There was only one small snag. On Mondays each child in the school had to bring a sum of money which would cover their school meals for a week. We often had as many as five of ours at St Joseph's at one time.

It would have been so easy for John just to write a cheque for the total sum required. But St Joseph's would have none of that. Every child had to bring an envelope with cash in it. Try as he might, John could never seem to have the correct amount of cash available. He would always top up what he had by raiding the kitties we were keeping for so many bridge friends. Then when dinner party time arrived the kitties would be stuffed with IOU notes, rather than cash so that the occasions tended to be expensive ones for us.

It was during this phase of our lives that I began to write. First were a couple of Catholic Truth Society pamphlets on marriage, on which I considered myself quite an authority until one family member who had better be nameless told me, 'Maureen, what you write is all pie in the sky.'

I was on the board of the CTS at the time and

naturally offered these thoughts without any expectation of payment. But I did feel a bit aggrieved when the then secretary of the CTS put a photograph of his daughter's marriage on the cover of the pamphlet, rather than asking if I would like to provide a photo of mine!

Nothing daunted, however, I added two more contributions about bringing up children, again rather conceitedly assuming that I was sufficiently experienced in that field for people to want to read what I thought about it.

These early writings were very largely scribbled on spare bits of paper while I was waiting for my children to complete their classes at the swimming baths. When I widened my audience and started to delve into humorous accounts of being a GP's wife, John insisted that he did not want his surname used, so my writing alias became Maureen Vincent, my two Christian names.

The wisdom of this became apparent when I wrote about the scandal that the NHS would pay for a practice nurse, unless that nurse happened to be the GP's wife, when it seemed to be assumed that claiming for her qualified services must be some kind of fraud on the part of the GP. As a solution to this common problem, I suggested, tongue in cheek, that Dr A's wife might like to swap nursing duties with Dr B's wife so that each could be paid their just salary.

What was my horror, minor compared to John's, to read an *Evening Standard* headline: *'Live In Sin Advises Doctor's Wife'* – setting out my cunning plan.

Gradually I began to contribute to magazines like

Woman's Realm and *Good Housekeeping*. I was also commissioned to write a piece for the first ever edition of *Cosmopolitan*.

One day John picked up a call from the editor of a women's publication. 'May I speak to Mrs Vincent?'

'Sorry,' said John completely forgetting what he had asked me to do, 'I'm afraid you have the wrong number.' The phone rang again and the request was repeated, as was John's rejection of it. The lady was persistent and rang a third time. 'I have Mrs Vincent's contact number in front of me.'

Light suddenly dawned. 'Oh, sorry, I forgot – she's my wife.'

I met a number of very interesting people through my freelance writing. The rudest person I encountered was Jimmy Savile. 'Where's your tape recorder?' he demanded, having kept me waiting a half an hour for our appointment. I explained that I would be taking the interview in shorthand.

'You'll *never* get *me* down in shorthand!'

Unfortunately I did.

Diana, the editor of *Woman's Realm* at the time, became a good friend and I was a regular contributor to her magazine. I liked doing profiles of celebrated people; she invariably accepted my suggestions for interviews.

Margaret Thatcher was someone who interested me very much. At the time she was at the Department of Education. I knew she had briefly practised as a barrister which was one reason for my interest. I suggested to Diana that I might do a profile of her and Diana agreed immediately on the proviso that I also interviewed Shirley Williams, another politician I was already keen to meet.

I was given an appointment to meet Margaret at her office. Then, a couple of days before the appointment, Diana phoned me. 'Sorry,' she told me, 'But the head of IPC says he won't touch Margaret Thatcher with a bargepole.'

Somehow my agent managed to get the commission transferred to another magazine. When I reached Margaret's office, the first thing I told her was that there had been a change of publication. 'Look,' she said to me. 'If you're having trouble placing this article, let's just sit here and have a coffee and a chat.'

And that's exactly what we did. She was relaxed and friendly, just as interested in my life as I was in hers, a real pleasure to talk to. When she heard I had passed my Bar exams she was the first person ever to say to me, 'But you have to use that when the children are older!'

Her boy and girl twins – another common factor in our lives – were in their teens at the time. I asked her how she was managing to juggle bringing up a family with her ministerial office.

'Just exactly the same as I'm sure you do with your seven,' she explained. 'I'm ironing at midnight with one eye on the television news.'

The article was due for publication several weeks later: a few days before the due date Margaret was elected leader of the Conservative Party in a shock defeat for Edward Heath.

She rang me the following day. 'The editor of the magazine has sent me the most beautiful bouquet of flowers,' she said. 'She should have sent them to you!'

I feel privileged to have seen a side of Margaret Thatcher which gets very little attention nowadays. No doubt power went to her head, as it invariably does in the end. And, for some reason the media have always had it in for her. When there was a procession through London on the occasion of her funeral, the broadcasters attempted to make out that few of the populace would bother to line the streets. The cameras proved them wrong.

In my opinion, Margaret Thatcher was one of the greatest prime ministers this country has ever had. The manner of her going was quite shameful. Despite the consistent attacks on her by the media, many of the electors saw in her what I saw, a thoroughly decent woman trying to do her best and achieving so much in the process. I am proud to have met her.

For the record, Shirley Williams was a lovely person too. Years later she came to give a talk at one of the oldest and best London clubs, where I was a member.

'Before I begin,' she insisted. 'I must just tell you of my first experience of this club.

'When I was a junior minister in the Labour Government I was involved in a government committee, the other members of which were all men. It was decided by them that our meetings would take place in this club, at a time when it did not admit women members.

'We met in an upstairs room, but I was not allowed to use the lift or the staircase; I was not even allowed through the front door. I was told to use the servants' entrance and the servants' staircase.

'When this club decided to admit women members, the secretary kindly wrote inviting me to join. I'm afraid I told him what to do with his invitation!'

Fascinating stuff, especially the choice of venue by the male members of Parliament on the committee, who would have been fully aware of the humiliation inflicted on their only female member.

It was certainly a man's world when Shirley Williams and I were entering the workplace, and most men at the time made sure that women knew it.

My friend Diana had progressed to becoming the female editor of *The Mail* and would occasionally invite me to make a contribution to her paper. At one time there was a big news story about a Catholic priest having refused to marry a couple because the prospective husband was disabled.

Diana called me. 'You are the only person who can tell me exactly what the Catholic position is on this story. Give me four hundred words.'

I called on a friend at Archbishop's House and he confirmed what I had thought: the priest concerned had made a crass theological mistake; there was no reason why the couple should not be married in the Catholic Church.

I dictated my four hundred words to Diana's secretary – no such thing as email in those days.

Diana rang me, 'Just what I want, thank you, but do you mind if I turn it into an interview with you as long as I keep strictly to what you have told me?' I had no objection because of course I could trust her.

But I had not expected that she would change what I had said into a double page feature with the screaming headline: *'What a Woman Knows That a Priest Doesn't – Maureen Mullally, Catholic Barrister and Family Lawyer Gives Us the Truth.'*

All I could think about was whether I was likely to be excommunicated or disbarred first. Luckily I escaped both.

That wasn't the only time I inspired headlines during my career. I was indeed a family law specialist, and had been in practice for several years in that speciality when one of my solicitors asked that I do something completely out of my comfort zone. His client had been the supervisor of a boys' home and had been taking some particularly unsuitable photographs of his young charges, undressed.

'He's pleading guilty of course,' the solicitor reassured me, 'but I want someone who looks like a mother and grandmother to mitigate for him.'

Feeling extremely doubtful about my ability to do so, I was persuaded by my clerks against my better judgment. Crime had not been my area as became apparent the moment I opened my mouth. An astonished judge heard me plead that what my client had done was not the worst he could have done in his position.

I do hope that this did not make my client's sentence any longer than it would have been, but my solicitor might at least have learned a valuable lesson about horses for courses. When I went down to commiserate with my client in the cells, he pleaded, 'Do you think the police would let me have my photographs back?' Even I knew that was not going to be an option.

When Nora and I got to the railway station for our commute the following day, I had to say, 'Nora, I'm on the front page of *The Times*!'

'Mummy,' she confirmed, 'You're on the front page of *all* the newspapers!'

My dear mother phoned that evening. 'Your name,' she informed me accusingly, 'was mentioned on television news today. Fortunately, they mis-pronounced it!'

I was then subjected to a lengthy cross-examination about whether all my cases were like that one. Mummy and Daddy were very displeased.

The whole incident simply confirmed my earlier conviction that I had never been cut out for the criminal Bar; thenceforward my clerks concurred, thank goodness.

- CHAPTER FOURTEEN -
PUPILLAGE

At the time when we realised I was expecting Mary Rose, John had been going through a nightmare experience. He had been sued for negligence by Mr B, an elderly patient who had suffered a leg amputation just below the knee. Mr B had been attending John's surgery regularly for treatment for bronchitis. John noticed that he was limping badly and asked if he could help.

Mr B assured him that his foot problem was being managed perfectly well by his chiropodist. John was still concerned and, on one occasion, actually managed to undo the lace on Mr B's heavy boot so that he could examine the foot. Mr B still refused point blank to allow John to go any further and insisted that his chiropodist was coping with whatever was wrong with it.

Then, one weekend John was called to Mr B's home by his family and discovered that the foot had become gangrenous and the gangrene had spread; there was no option but to perform surgery to remove his lower leg. Mr B's family consulted a solicitor about suing the chiropodist. But it turned out that the chiropodist had minimal insurance. The solicitor advised the family to sue John too.

Fortunately John was absolutely meticulous about

record keeping. Each visit noted on Mr B's card described a consultation about his bronchitis, with no mention of his foot since John had never been allowed to examine it.

When the court papers were served on John he consulted his medical insurance company.

When the solicitor advising him had examined the records, he told John that there was no chance that Mr B's claim would be successful.

But when Mr B's legal advisers had the records disclosed to them they persisted with his claim. In those days cases like this could drag on and on before coming to court. Nowadays every case has a timetable set by a judge and failure to get on with the case means automatic dismissal. John's bad luck was that Mr B's claim was so obviously going to fail that the Medical Defence Union decided to contest it. Ironically, had he been at fault, the insurers would have negotiated to settle the claim by payment of a sum of money.

So we had about two years of purgatory, with delays so protracted that we would allow ourselves to hope that the case might have gone away, only to be contacted again with the news that it was going ahead. John, always a worrier, was having sleepless nights. If Mr B won the case, he explained to me, it would affect Seán as much as it affected him, since some patients would be bound to leave the practice when it became public. Even if Mr B didn't win, patients would say to themselves, 'No smoke without fire', believing that John would have been lucky to get away with something.

When we finally got to the High Court, it was the

feast of St Jude, the patron saint of hopeless cases, to whom I had been praying. 'Don't ever mention St Jude to me again,' John warned as we walked across Westminster Bridge *en route* to his ordeal.

His insurers had instructed leading counsel. Mr B limped into the witness box supported by his stick and confirmed his name and address. The first question his barrister asked was, 'When was the first time you consulted Dr Mullally about your foot?'

Mr B banged his stick on the floor of the box and replied, 'How many times do I have to tell people that I *never* consulted Dr Mullally about my foot!'

'I think you might like to take instructions,' the judge advised his barrister.

Instructions having been taken, the barrister informed the court that his client would be withdrawing his claim against John.

That was not the only miracle worked that day. Where there are two defendants in a case they are listed in alphabetical order; the chiropodist's surname was ahead of John's in the alphabet, so that John was simply described as 'another'.

Cases against medical defendants are always popular with the 'stringers', reporters who check court lists and inform local newspapers in the doctor's area of practice. This is what John had been so concerned about.

But we were outside the courtroom before anyone had a chance to spot that a doctor was involved in the case. So no reports in the local press. John changed his mind about St Jude after that. But the whole affair took its toll on him, nevertheless.

*

Eight years later, when Hugh was coming up to eighteen and Mary Rose up to eight, John dropped his bombshell. He had a habit of mulling things over very carefully before I was invited to share any plan. I never minded that although I think some modern wives might.

'When are you thinking of starting to practise at the Bar?'

'Don't be ridiculous,' was my first reaction, 'I haven't opened a law book for fifteen years!'

'Well,' he persisted, 'I've been giving it some thought. I have women patients ten years older than you regretting that they never took up a career they were trained for when they had the chance.'

I was not impressed. I was enjoying looking after the children, writing and occasionally broadcasting on the radio. I had a very full life already.

'John, you know I only took the exams to prove Daddy wrong. I'm perfectly happy with my life now and I'll never have any regrets.'

Then came the killer argument. 'It would give me a night's sleep if I thought you had an income if anything happened to me.'

I knew he was a worrier. Since the Mr B affair he had not been a good sleeper – not a problem I ever experienced. 'Maureen could sleep on a harrow,' he would boast. I don't know that I ever saw a harrow, but realised that it was a very uncomfortable farm implement familiar to him from his childhood.

If I could relieve him of some of his sleepless nights I would certainly try to do what he was recommending.

I honestly didn't think there was the slightest chance of my being accepted for pupillage, an essential preliminary to practice at the Bar. But if it would make John happier I would certainly try.

The first step would be to make an appointment with the Under Treasurer of Gray's Inn, to see if he could be of any help. The interview did not go well. Having ascertained that I had seven children, he expressed doubts as grave as my own and told me, for good measure, that he himself had married a girl who was studying for the Bar exams and she had never even taken them.

However, not wishing to put a complete damper on my ambitions, he gave me the name of a distinguished woman who was a criminal silk, who might advise me. She kindly agreed to meet me, listened to my tale patiently and said, 'My advice to you, my dear, is to go home and look after your seven children!'

My last hope was dear Anne Curnow, whose lecture notes had enabled me to get through the last year of my degree without leaving baby Hugh for one lecture or tutorial. She herself was already a silk (Queen's Counsel) and a highly regarded criminal practitioner.

'Let's face it, my dear,' was her verdict, 'the only thing you know anything about is the family so we'll have to find you a family practitioner.'

And she did. Margaret Booth was a contemporary of ours at University College – the law faculties were so small in those days that King's, UC and London School of Economics all shared lectures. Margaret was already a star of the Family Law Division; in fact I was to be her last pupil as she took silk at the end of my pupillage. QCs do not take pupils.

Margaret went on to become only the third woman to be appointed a High Court Judge, after Elizabeth Lane and Rose Heilbron.

When Elizabeth was first appointed she was going on circuit to hear cases at an important venue away from London. High Court Judges were always accompanied by young barristers called 'marshals', who are basically there to smooth the path for them, serve drinks at social events they are holding and act as general dogsbodies.

Elizabeth was sitting quietly knitting in a corner of the first-class carriage reserved for her when her marshal burst into it. 'Madam, I'm afraid I must ask you to leave at once. This carriage is reserved for a High Court Judge.'

'Young man,' she informed him, looking at him over her spectacles, 'I *am* the High Court Judge.'

Years later Nora, who had been called to the Bar, was kindly invited by Margaret to be her marshal on circuit. The lodgings for the judges were magnificent properties, well staffed and comfortably furnished. A couple of days after their arrival Margaret was hosting a dinner party for local worthies. She told Nora that her job would be to serve the *aperitifs*.

'But I don't know how much tonic water people take in their whiskey,' Nora panicked.

'Don't worry, dear, we'll just have champagne.'

This was the first time Nora had been away from home without us. Naturally I phoned on the first night to make sure things were going well for her. The butler answered my call; I explained that I would like to speak to Miss Mullally. 'To whom, Madam?'

'My daughter, Nora Mullally, the Judge's Marshal.'

'Oh, had you said the Judge's Marshal I would have known,' he informed me grandly.

That night, on her way to bed, Nora passed a bowl of fruit and helped herself to an apple. The butler told her that an apple was missing and she had to confess. But for all the remaining nights of her stay she found an apple ready, together with a knife and a napkin, on a plate in her room.

Margaret was celebrated not only for her skill as a barrister, but also for the work she had been doing for several years on *Rayden*, the family law Bible for all practitioners in the field. In response to her arguments, High Court Judges, even those in the Court of Appeal, would say, 'Oh well, Miss Booth, you wrote the book!'

It was more than generous of her to have taken me on in my ignorant state. She was immensely encouraging too and kept me on for nine months, rather than the usual six, to give me more of a chance to catch up with the other pupils in chambers, all just finished with university and the Bar exams.

I needed encouragement. My first day as a pupil was one of the loneliest I had ever spent; the other pupils went off for lunch together but it did not occur to them to include someone almost old enough to be their mother. I wandered along Chancery Lane, looking for somewhere to get a sandwich and asking myself what on earth I was doing there. The first task I had been given that morning was to draft a divorce petition.

We then went over Fleet Street to the High Court where Margaret's client was a petitioner for divorce. In those days divorce petitions had to be heard by a judge, nowadays they are usually a paper exercise. Margaret introduced me to her client; as she did so, I looked at the woman, astonished in my own mind, 'She's getting divorced today and she's not even crying!'

Shows you how much I didn't know. Only one of my friends had been divorced before I started my pupillage.

We went back to chambers and Margaret gave me a second petition to draft. When I handed it to her she said, 'Maureen, you're *still* making the same mistake,' which I thought was pretty hard since it was only my second go and it was only a single error – she'd told me about at least a dozen others on the first one.

Kind though she was, I soon discovered that Margaret was a perfectionist. She taught me to be a perfectionist too. It had been a long day and I left to go home unconvinced that this was what I should be doing at all. How would the family manage without me during the day?

In fact, it turned out that the family were managing very well. John would be home at the times when they returned from school. The children told me, 'We are getting to know Daddy so much better.'

Hugh expressed his satisfaction. 'Mummy, you're so much broader minded now.'

Well, I no longer lay awake waiting for him to come home when he'd been out with his friends. I was realising how many mothers had much greater concerns to live with.

Mary Rose informed a fascinated Reverend Mother that 'Mummy's gone back to her old work as a bar maid.'

And at the end of the first week I found on my pillow a bath cube, carefully wrapped in gift paper by her, with a note which said: 'You must be so tired that you need a lovely bath.'

Margaret's fellow members of chambers were men, although one of the other pupils was female. The chambers clerk was one of the old school, to the point where the only female barrister he would acknowledge was Margaret. Throughout my pupillage he invariably addressed me as 'Sir'. The head of chambers made sure that I realised there was no hope of a tenancy for me by reminding me every time he came across me that I would be leaving on the date arranged.

I was still very unsure that I ought to be pursuing a career at the Bar. On one occasion we were sitting outside court, when Margaret would no doubt have been preoccupied with the case she was about to deal with. Selfishly, I started to tell her of my doubts. 'Look,' she told me. 'You are keeping to the hours you must keep to as a pupil. When you get a tenancy you won't be in court all that often at first and you'll have much more time with the family.'

The hours were not the only problem. I needed a second six month pupillage and I did not know how to find one. 'You *must* know another barrister,' Margaret insisted.

The only one I knew was Stanislaus Seuffert, head of his own chambers, and a fellow member of a school board of governors. Margaret knew him of course, and it occurs to me now that she may have put a word in for me; she certainly insisted that I approach him.

Full of trepidation, I asked for an interview appointment. Dear Stanislaus; he arranged a pupillage for me with a Jewish member of his chambers, Aron Owen. Stanislaus also reassured me about something which I had been seeing as a problem. How could a Catholic represent someone in divorce proceedings?

He explained that divorce law applies to the state element of a marriage. Representing one of the parties, if they happen to have been married in a church, does not affect the validity of the religious marriage. For a Catholic, for example, the validation of a marriage can be tested in the diocesan tribunals. For someone who is Jewish the religious element of the marriage has to be dissolved by a 'Get'.

One of the prominent silks in family law in my early days was Anita Ryan, who was a Catholic. I was led by her in the Appeal Court on at least one occasion. She was a memorable lady who tended to address Appeal Court judges as 'My DEAH' rather than according them the usual 'My Lord'.

On our appeal, one of their Lordships committed an error. When our opponents had put their case, this unfortunate judge, perhaps anxious to adjourn for lunch said, 'We needn't trouble you, Miss Ryan.'

This would usually have meant that we had won, since obviously both sides must have the opportunity to put their case. However, the court then went on to dismiss our appeal. Incandescent, Anita rose, magisterially, to her full height: 'I *must* protest, my

DEAH!'

The unfortunate judge had been Anita's pupil master, which made the situation even worse. 'Just tell me what you want, Miss Ryan,' he pleaded, abject.

She won her opportunity to put her case but they still, rather bravely, found against us.

When I met John aged twenty-one.

My brother Jimmy.

Marriage to John, August 1953. With my parents, Oonagh and Mike.

The family, 1960s.

John qualifies, 1945.

Pursuing a career at the Bar, late 1970s.

John and I on holiday in Ireland in the 1990s.

At my retirement dinner in Middle Temple, 2000.

Neil and I engaged, 2011.

Grandchildren in Ireland for John's 75th birthday: 1994.
back row: (l to r) Siobhán, Alex, James,
Tom with Rósín, Katie, Fiona with Georgia;
front: John with Ciarán, Will, Tara.

Marriage to Neil, with our ten children, sixteen grandchildren and other relations.

With Oonagh and Mike on my seventy-fifth birthday.

(l to r) Adrian and Katie, Nora, James and Mary Rose, Tom, Hugh, Maureen, Margaret, Alice and Pat.

Rosie having family hug with Mary Rose and James.

John and Charlotte..

Fiona and Andy.

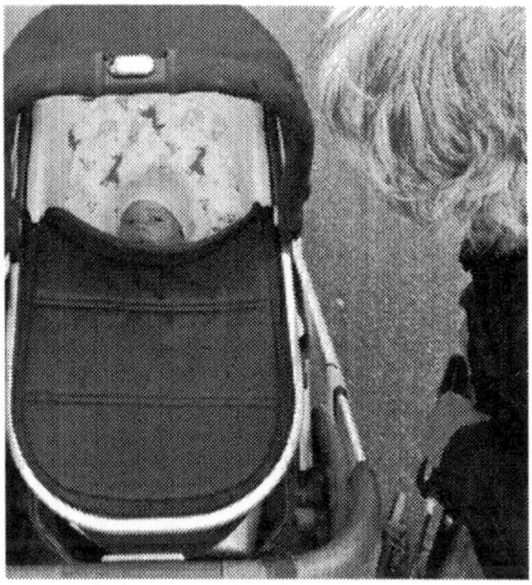

Arlo meeting his great-granny.

Tom and Aoife.

Thirteen grandchildren May 2017 – [l to r] back row: Will, Ciarán, Alex, Siobhán, Fiona, Tom, Katie and John; front row: James, Rosie, Tara, Rósín and Georgia.

My ninetieth birthday.

- CHAPTER FIFTEEN -
FIRST STEPS AT THE BAR

My second pupil master, Aron Owen, was a recognised authority on the Rent Acts, not an area of the law in which I had any ambition to specialise. He did, however, also venture into family law cases and felt that, having spent nine months in Margaret's august presence, I should be of some assistance to him in that aspect of his work.

He was a very kind man, but his approach to the court was as far away from Margaret's breezy and well-earned confidence as it could possibly have been. When going into court, even for cases on which he was an acknowledged expert, he would literally shake with nerves. One of my principal duties was to calm him down. Once inside the court his expertise took over and he was widely respected among the judiciary, eventually being appointed a circuit judge himself.

Aron was Jewish, as were most members of chambers. Judges would always respect the necessity for devout Jews to be home before darkness fell on Friday nights and would adjourn hearings at an early hour to facilitate them. The chambers clerk Stanley remarked to me once that if you weren't in court on the Day of Atonement then you didn't have a practice; there would be no Jewish barristers in court on that day.

In your second six you are allowed to appear in court. chambers clerks find small cases in the magistrates' courts for baby barristers to cut their teeth on. My first such exercise was completely terrifying. Before that I had been in a magistrates' court on one occasion only. Margaret's practice was confined to the High Court, the Court of Appeal and the House of Lords. However, on this particular day a magistrate had made an order relating to one of her clients with which she profoundly disagreed.

Joe Jackson, head of chambers, accompanied us to the East End in a black cab. Joe put the magistrates right, the order was rescinded and we all piled into another cab back to chambers. Nowadays students for the Bar exams and pupils get so much intensive training that no one could possibly be as ignorant as I was then.

Heart in my mouth, I joined the other lawyers waiting for their cases to be called on. Every one of them would be hoping that theirs would be one of the first in the list. I sat there praying that mine would be the last, watching exactly what each one ahead of me said and did so that I could pick up what to do when my turn came. With Margaret the court was invariably being addressed as 'My Lord' or 'My Lady'. Try as I might to remember to say 'sir' or 'madam' in the magistrates' court, the more elevated address could occasionally escape me to the obvious astonishment of the tribunal and the amused smiles of the lawyers.

Until then I had led an extremely sheltered life – I

had only met one criminal. Before Nora was born we were friendly with a number of young couples with children of similar ages. Among them were the Browns. Dick was an Australian naval officer posted to London. He and his wife Pat rented a ground floor flat and introduced us all to the occupants of the flat above them, who had two little boys.

We shared children's parties and dinner parties and knew one another really well. The father of the little boys was a very uncommunicative man, however. I didn't dislike him but had an uncomfortable feeling that he considered himself possibly too intellectual to be bothered with people like us. He said little and seemed to prefer watching the rest of us with a slightly disapproving air.

I was still in hospital after Nora's birth when the front page of my newspaper delivered the shock:

George Blake, for he it was, had been arrested and charged with spying for the Russians. All the world now knows the story, how he had been a double agent working for our secret service as well, how he had been able to communicate information to the Russians which resulted in the deaths of many of our own agents, how he was eventually sentenced to forty-two years in prison, escaped with the help of the IRA and ended up living in Moscow.

I felt so sorry for his wife. I imagine she would have had no idea. We felt desperately sorry for Dick too. Clearly his friendship with Blake must have placed him under suspicion with the Australian authorities.

Stanley, the chambers clerk, continued to have a touching faith in my ability which I felt was completely unjustified. And now my second six was nearing its close. Stanislaus invited me to his room to discuss my future. I told him of course that I hoped to practise. 'That's just what I wanted to discuss with you. I've been thinking and I feel it might be more appropriate for you to apply to my friend Hume Boggis-Rolfe for a job in the Lord Chancellor's Office. As a junior barrister, you know, you would be expected to travel all over the country to magistrates' courts at very short notice and the clerks would be reluctant to ask you to do that.'

I was deeply disappointed about his suggestion but there was no option but to agree to attend the appointment Stanislaus had made with this very grand gentleman. At the time he was deputy secretary in the LCO, but went on to even greater heights. In 2002 he was appointed to head the new Law Commission, a body set up to implement the reform and modernisation of the law of England and Wales.

At the interview I found him to be an intimidating presence. However, to my considerable surprise, he did offer me a job, probably on the basis that I was a proficient shorthand typist rather than with any expectation that I would be showing much legal promise. I returned to chambers determined to have another go at changing Stanislaus' mind. I would never refuse to go anywhere the clerks wanted me to go, I told him, and they should just treat me as they would any beginner.

Somewhat to my surprise I found I had a good deal of support. The two senior women in chambers, Valerie Pearlman and Fiona Stoll, spoke up for me telling

Stanislaus that I was invariably punctual as a pupil and willing to do anything anyone asked me to do.

Stanley, too, was on my side which was very important. He told Stanislaus that he would much prefer to take me on than a young girl who would only get married and have children as soon as he had built up her practice. Those arguments won the day for me and Stanislaus reluctantly agreed to take me on.

Ours was a general common law set, meaning that we practised in criminal law, family law, immigration law, contract, tort and almost anything else solicitors could throw at us. At the time there were only about eleven members, the atmosphere was informal and anything but competitive, which larger specialised sets tended to be.

About five o'clock in the evening the junior members who were not in court on the following day would congregate outside the clerk's room, hoping for a late brief.

'Early days,' Stanley would say to keep up our spirits, in the hope that the phone would ring. Sometimes it did.

One late calling solicitor needed one of us urgently the following day. I could hear Stanley's end of the conversation, 'Yes, I know she's a woman but we haven't any men free tomorrow.'

Such was the prejudice which could still be openly demonstrated. On the day of my call to the Bar, Gray's Inn had presented all the newly called with a book entitled *Duty and Art in Advocacy* by the Hon. Sir Malcolm Hilbery, a Justice of the King's Bench Division, published in 1946.

It was not until I was glancing through it recently that I realised that every barrister mentioned was either 'he' or 'him'; this despite the fact that Helena Normanton, the first woman to practise at the Bar had been called in 1922, twenty-four years before its publication.

While we waited hopefully for a last minute set of instructions, a couple of the senior barristers might be practising their putting on the hall carpet. Two who shared a room close to the clerks had a pleasant habit of finding a bottle of wine in one of their filing cabinets and inviting people in to have a glass.

I will be frank. I was never any good at crime. I invariably believed what my clients told me. Mary Rose became a solicitor and laboured under the same illusion until the day she came home, dropped her briefcase on the kitchen floor, helped herself to a restorative glass of wine and admitted gloomily, 'They've all done it, Mummy.'

There was my Irish client who had been growing cannabis in his large attic. He told me (and I accepted) that he owned a parrot and had decided to see whether the seed it consumed would grow into anything. When I made this compelling submission in court the judge raised his eyes to heaven and asked me whether I had seen the photographic results of this 'interesting experiment'.

Not only was the poor guy sentenced to a term of imprisonment, he was to be deported back to Ireland afterwards.

A kind friend who had retired handed on to me his gown and his horsehair wig. Usually the beginner's wig and gown in their pristine state proclaim inexperience right away – my wig had been round the track for years and looked it, especially after Lucy our springer spaniel, (clearly and understandably under the impression that it was a rat!) had got hold of it one day and shaken it so vigorously that some of the curls became permanently detached.

I was in my forties so in that wig could pass for an experienced practitioner – that is, until I opened my mouth. During the luncheon adjournment in one of my first criminal cases, the court usher informed me that the judge wanted to see me. I quaked. What had I done?

He started off by telling me that he had looked up my date of call – 1957 – it was then well into the 1970s. I could see his problem so admitted that I had only recently started to practise. 'I thought that might be the case,' he told me, 'so now I'm going to give you a few hints about cross examining a police officer.'

Which he did. And I was more than grateful.

Gradually I began to acquire some confidence and to enjoy the discreet fun to be had in counsel's row while the judge dealt with other cases. Dress was very important. Margaret had decreed that my engagement ring, a small sapphire surrounded by even smaller diamonds, was 'too showy' for court so that had to go in a drawer at home and be replaced beside my wedding ring by another plain gold one.

In those days, women barristers never wore trousers unless, like one poor girl I knew, they had had a skiing accident and couldn't wear a skirt while the leg healed.

The rules for men were very strict too. The hapless

male sitting on my right was told by a judge, 'I can't see you, Mr X.' I stared. He looked perfectly obvious to me.

The usher handed him a note from the judge: 'You are wearing a blue shirt.'

The young man had to make a hasty exit to find himself a white shirt.

Another time I glanced at the name on the brief belonging to another young man who was opposing me in a case and realised that he was the baby brother of one of my school friends. I handed him a note: 'The last time we met I was helping to give you a bath.'

That put him off his stroke for a few minutes.

Once in the women's robing room a very senior lady began to sniff suspiciously. 'Someone,' she declared in forbidding tones, 'is wearing *perfume*.'

I was very glad it wasn't me.

On one occasion I had to make a hasty exit to find a legal outfitters myself. Stanislaus was leading me in a case and when I had arrived at the High Court accused me of not wearing 'weepers'. I had no idea what he was talking about but was despatched to find them at once.

The shop assistant was able to put me right.

A minor royal had died the previous day and it was the custom to wear special bands to demonstrate our grief. The bands are the double collar all barristers wear round their necks. I wonder if weepers still get worn. Probably not. In fact, I don't know whether barristers even robe anymore!

My Crown Court case with the taking and driving away merchants finally convinced Stanley that I was going to be more suited to the Family Division than the criminal fraternity. Still very much learning on my feet, I gradually acquired more self-confidence and really began to enjoy my practice. My friends in chambers became like a second family.

In those days barristers shared rooms in chambers. I ended up in a magnificent bow-windowed room overlooking Middle Temple garden and down to the Thames.

The other two occupants were a Jewish dentist who practised both professions simultaneously, quite a feat, and a young man who eventually became an Anglican vicar, so our room was pretty ecumenical. We became close friends who respected our different faiths.

At home, one of my grandchildren was helping me to make the bed one day.

'Granny' she said looking round our bedroom, 'where are they?'

'Who, love?'

'The people who share your room.'

Well, she had obviously overheard me talking about John and Tony.

- CHAPTER SIXTEEN - ME AND THE BBC

I began contributing talks to BBC *Woman's Hour* in the years when I was at home looking after John and the family, and had begun contributing to women's magazines. The programme had started in 1946 – with a male presenter, Alan Ivimey, appointed because it was felt that a female 'might be resented' by listeners.

A few months later, however, that surprising appointee had been replaced by a female; all subsequent presenters have been female.

The programme has run continuously for over seventy years and is the longest running radio programme for women in the world. In my day the two outstanding women presenters were Marjorie Anderson and Sue McGregor.

Unsurprisingly, the first piece I submitted to *Woman's Hour* was about my granny, who brought me up until I was seven years old. I was absolutely thrilled when I was invited to Broadcasting House to read it. At that time the programme was in the afternoon, so I received an invitation to lunch with the producer, the presenter and my fellow contributors at the BBC.

Before lunch we all had a rehearsal. The delicious meal was served in a private room on a dining table clothed with an immaculate white tablecloth adorned with matching napkins, pretty china and gleaming cutlery. I was offered a glass of wine to accompany the meal. I turned that down because I was so nervous.

'Oh, you must have a glass,' I was told. 'It will relax you and your voice will sound much better.'

I wonder if today's contributors are treated quite so generously. The wine did have a calming effect on my nerves and I was never the slightest bit scared of broadcasting after that.

At about the time when I had just become a member of chambers the BBC sent me an invitation to join a training session lasting a week in order to familiarise myself with the operation of the Uher reel-to-reel tape recorder, with a view, I suppose to inviting me to become an interviewer myself.

I accepted the invitation and turned up to find that I was one of eight people in the class, one of whom was Jan Leeming who went on to become a news reading star of broadcasting. As far as I remember, the others were all men.

The Uher was an awkward piece of equipment, large and heavy, not at all easy to operate. However, I mastered it pretty well, as did all the others on the course. After a week, our final test was that we should take our Uher from Broadcasting House, find someone to interview on an interesting topic and produce the recording to our tutor.

I decided that I would interview dear Leonard Krikler, our newly appointed head of chambers, following on Stanislaus' retirement. Approached, he kindly agreed that I might interview him on the subject of what he thought about women at the Bar – there were few enough of us in those days to make his views interesting.

At the appointed hour I arrived in his room carrying my Uher, an inconveniently clumsy burden, and set it up on his desk between us. Switching on the recording, I started on my carefully worked out questions. But to my surprise Lennie began to shove his chair backwards, away from his desk and further away from me. 'What's the matter?' I wanted to know.

'Maureen, why are you leering at me in that sinister manner?'

'Lennie, I'm smiling at you encouragingly – it's what we're trained to do.'

Whereupon we both collapsed into gales of giggles, and that was the end of the interview.

For the moment.

We had to have another go when we could manage to keep our faces straight and our voices from wobbling.

I did complete the course successfully but, having thought about it carefully, realised that my career had come to a fork in the road. There was no way I could practise at the Bar if I were to accept an offer from the BBC. Much as I would have loved to do so, I had spent years qualifying as a lawyer and I should concentrate on that.

My daughter Nora was doing a temporary job with a Catholic newspaper at about the same time. She was given a Uher to take with her to a press conference given by Cardinal Hume on his return from a visit to a famine-blighted country in Africa.

When it came to her turn to ask a question she managed to let the machine slip from her lap where it landed on the polished floor and skated over to the Cardinal's feet.

Courteously, he retrieved it and handed it back to her. 'And your question?'

Nora's planned question had gone out of her head, she was so embarrassed by the unconcealed amusement of the other representatives of the media.

'What effect did it have on you, seeing all those starving people?' she blurted.

'That is something which I am not really prepared to talk about,' the Cardinal replied sadly. And he proceeded to the next questioner.

My broadcasting career had not come to a complete standstill after the Uher training, however. Jimmy Young, a popular presenter, had his own show every morning on BBC2. Somehow or other, I became his go-to commentator on any aspect of family law which was hitting the headlines.

A colleague rang me up to say, 'I was driving to court this morning and heard your voice on the radio. I nearly drove up a telephone pole!'

Jimmy was a delightful host, always kind and appreciative. He had started off as a popular singer, with now long forgotten hits like *The Man from Laramie* and *Unchained Melody.*

I was still having articles published in magazines like *Good Housekeeping* and was commissioned to do a piece for the very first publication of *Cosmopolitan*. I had to interview a gentleman, with no medical qualifications as far as I recall, who was making a fortune by injecting cells from young lambs into ladies with more money than sense, on a promise that the treatment would rejuvenate them.

I was actually quite impressed by his claims but, needless to say, when I attempted to persuade John of their efficacy, he was derisive.

It was not easy to keep up the writing for magazines either, working in chambers as a pupil from 9am until 6pm five days a week; the additional time commuting in the rush hour trains, often without a seat; having to cook dinner for ten of us, including the *au pair*, every night; planning lunch for the following day; and trying to fit in my role as wife and mother between all the other commitments. On top of all that, John and I didn't want to miss out on our social life with our friends on the golf course and at dinner parties, some of which we hosted ourselves.

Small wonder then that at times during my pupillages I sometimes felt exhausted and a bit despondent. On one such occasion Margaret and I were waiting to go into court for a hearing on one of her cases in Somerset House, in the Strand. At that time this historic and stunningly beautiful property was being used to accommodate hearings by registrars in divorce suits – such a desecration.

While we waited, I confided in Margaret for the second time that I really did not know if I should keep on with the idea of eventually being able to practise at the Bar on my own account. It did seem as though there were far too many obstacles. Margaret, kindness itself as always, would not hear a word about my giving up, having come so far already.

Once I had finished pupillage and been given a seat in chambers, I would find things so much easier, she explained. I would have very few cases of my own to begin with, and would no longer be tied to the everyday routine of long hours necessitated by pupillage. She took the trouble to talk me out of my plan to give up, and I shall always be grateful for that.

It was hard for John too, as I had envisaged that it would be when he made his suggestion that I should find pupillages. But, being the person he was, he never gave up on his unwavering support for me. He helped the children, especially the younger ones, to adapt to my absence by spending more time with them than he had done previously, with consequent enjoyment and closer relationships on both sides. He was the one waiting for them when they got home from school, as he usually had a few hours between lunch and his evening surgery, so he was now the one to get all the news about their days first. I found myself taking a bit of a back seat, but as long as he and the children were happy, we all settled into our new way of family life without, I hope, too much disruption.

One of my daughters commented perceptively that he reminded her of the then popular song, *You Are the Wind Beneath my Wings.*

One of her sisters corrected her and said the song she thought described Dad's attitude to me was, *Just the Way You Are.*'

When we eventually lost him, one of the girls said to Oonagh, 'Mummy and Daddy were one of the great love stories.'

A compliment I really cherish.

- CHAPTER SEVENTEEN -
MY FIRST PUPIL

During my early years as a practitioner I did not share Stanley's burgeoning confidence in my abilities. I dreaded the moment when I had to open my case, wondering whether I would ever feel as confident and relaxed as, it seemed to me, the other barristers around me in counsel's row.

For my first appearance in the county court, representing the petitioner in an undefended divorce, I tried to reflect Margaret's approach as closely as possible. It would be difficult if not impossible to lose an undefended case, but I suspected that I might even achieve that impossibility.

My client, the petitioner, was if anything as terrified as I was. In faithful imitation of my revered pupil master, having heard her take the oath to tell the truth and nothing but the truth, I advised, 'Now, do try to keep your voice up so that His Honour can hear you.'

'Yes, do,' agreed the learned judge, 'and it might encourage Mrs Mullally to keep *her* voice up so that I can hear *her*!'

That particular judge, who had better remain nameless, had a habit of starting off by informing hapless counsel that he had read the papers and come to the following conclusion, unless either of us had anything to say to convince him otherwise. All very well if he had decided in your favour but a bit of a downer if he hadn't.

On one occasion my opponent was a young man from my own chambers. The application I was making was being heard in private in the judge's room at the back of the courtroom. The judge had, happily, revealed that he had decided in my favour, when my opposite number banged his fist on the table where we were sitting and shouted, 'It's not fair – she *always wins!*'

'We all have days like that, Mr X,' was the judge's soothing response.

High Court judges could be equally idiosyncratic. One had been wounded in the leg on war service and had a most disconcerting habit of leaving his doubtless uncomfortable seat on the bench and prowling up and down in front of it while he heard the case. You'd glance down at your papers and never know where to find him when you looked up.

But he was a helpful tribunal. An essential part of a divorce petition is the 'acknowledgment of service' document which proves that the respondent to the petition has seen and signed it.

In one of my cases the respondent husband had become so incensed when he saw the contents of the petition that he simply wrote a very rude word on the acknowledgment, crushed it in his fist and threw it into the waste paper basket. No signature of course.

I handed up this inadequate document and the judge read the rude word. 'Does she recognise the handwriting?' he asked sympathetically. She got her divorce.

In those days all divorce petitions had to be heard by a judge. The petitioner had to prove her (it was usually her) case, which meant that she had to repeat in oral evidence the reasons for which she was seeking a divorce, which would have been clearly set out in the petition itself.

This was known as 'coming up to proof'. I had one unfortunate lady who was so nervous that she completely failed to give the necessary evidence. Counsel are not permitted to 'lead' their clients, so there was no way I could give her a hint. This was a petition based on the 'unreasonable behaviour' of the husband.

When I had three separate times asked her about a date on which one of the examples of bad behaviour had occurred, without her having given any sign of recollection of what had taken place on that date, I was getting desperate.

But my dear prowling judge walked over to the witness box and helped me out: 'Now, madam, *you* know what happened on that date. Your counsel knows what happened. But the silly old judge doesn't know, so *you* have to tell him!'

That did the trick.

So often in those first few years I would return to chambers in the depths of depression. I had lost a case again. It must have been my fault. I did win some, of course, and on one such occasion I returned elated because the outcome had been good.

Lennie invited me into his room and told me to sit down. 'Now, Maureen,' he said. 'Next time you lose a case, please promise me to think about today and not be so downcast.'

It was good and helpful advice. The other members of my set were all equally supportive. If things were looking dodgy for one of us in a case in the High Court, just across the Strand, everyone who chanced to be in chambers at the luncheon adjournment would help by suggesting and looking up some authority on the point which might be of assistance.

My confidence in myself was improving. At last I was able to convince myself that there was a winner and a loser in every case – and to lose a case was not necessarily my fault.

Some solicitors were actually asking for me to take their cases now, rather than the clerks simply allocating me work which some senior member was unable to take on.

One day Lennie came to me with his own problem. Stanislaus, our former head of chambers, a Catholic himself, had asked Leonard to interview the first – and probably still the only – nun who had been called to the Bar. As a Jew, Lennie explained, he had, unsurprisingly, never met a nun in his life. Would I sit in on the interview as a favour to him?

In view of his many kindnesses to me, it was obviously the least I could do. Unsuspectingly, I happily agreed.

Sister Mary More had been the principal of a highly successful high school for girls until her recent retirement. She was an imposing authoritative lady, dressed in ordinary clothes rather than a nun's habit, and wished to be called by her baptismal name Christina. Stanley, himself a Catholic, observed on a later occasion that 'You could dress Christina in anything you like but she'd still look like a nun.'

On her retirement as head teacher, Sister Mary More had received a lump sum from the local authority operating the school; to the consternation of her community she had announced that she was going to use it to train to be a barrister rather than follow the usual course of donating it to the community funds. She wasn't the sort of person people argued with, so here she was.

Stanislaus, I was told, had sent her to Lennie so that he could gently explain to her the impossibility of her getting a pupillage.

When we had discussed the difficulties in her path for about twenty minutes Lennie dropped his bombshell. 'Maureen, why don't you take Christina on as your first pupil?'

With the advantage of hindsight, I now realise that Stanislaus had plotted this with Lennie and that together they had decided that to take me by surprise would be the best tactic. It was quite impossible for me to refuse with Christina sitting there with pleading eyes, and when I knew I was her only hope. So I had been ambushed.

Christina came to join me on the following Monday. In the morning I gave her papers to read in a case where I had a conference with client and solicitor that afternoon. Come the appointed time, I introduced her as my pupil, believing that the introduction would be her last intervention in the proceedings, as was the custom with pupils.

But I had not allowed for Christina's habit of

authority. Apart from any other consideration she was about ten years older than me and used to having her views taking precedence over those of her staff. Startled, I had to listen as she embarked on how she saw matters and what her advice to my client would be. Somehow we got through the conference when I managed to take over control, taking my leave of a very surprised solicitor and, unfortunately, a slightly baffled client, since the advice I was giving was not in accord with Christina's.

It was probably one of the bravest things I had done in my life but, as soon as my door had closed behind them, I had to explain to this indomitable lady that my clients would be coming to hear what I had to say about their cases, and that she should be an attentive and silent listener, able to make suggestions and have discussions afterwards.

I will say that, once the realities of her role had been explained, Christina developed into a loyal and hardworking pupil. We became very good friends and spent an enjoyable six months together. One day I had a case in the appeal court – always a terrifying experience: three of the brightest brains in the country batting you around the court often, it appeared to me, for their private amusement. 'Is that your best point, Mrs Mullally?'

So I was outside waiting for my case to be called and preparing it over and over in my mind, with Christina hopping from foot to foot in excitement: her first case in the appeal court!

'Could I just go in and see what's going on?'

'Do, Christina.' (And give me a chance to

concentrate).

But in five minutes she was out again. 'You'll never *guess* who is in that court!'

Wearily: 'Who, Christina?'

'Mick Jagger!'

The reader will have to make allowances for me. My mind was completely on my coming ordeal when I replied, 'Whose chambers is he in?'

That was a case I won. 'Little did their lordships know there were three convents praying against them,' Christina explained triumphantly.

Christina had an elderly little car. I have to admit that it was a great convenience when going to and from courts outside London. But my heart was often in my mouth as she drove along, turning to me in conversation, without paying any apparent attention to where the car was supposed to be heading. Very sadly, she was killed a few years later when she drove it the wrong way onto a motorway.

Over my career I enjoyed the company of many pupils. Fiona, a lovely girl from Northern Ireland, has been a life-long friend. We met after a dinner in Middle Temple; John was with me. Fiona had lost a challenge and been ordered to sing by the senior in hall who must have known that she had a beautiful voice.

I can still remember the song she chose: *The Town I Loved So Well.*

When it ended John suggested that I ask Fiona to join us. She had not been able to find a pupillage so I offered her one on the spot. She was always full of fun and very enterprising. There was the time when she was due to meet her second pupil master at court with essential papers for his case and had arrived at the local station to find that there were no taxis available. Fiona spotted a lorry park across the road, ran over to the café there and enquired whether any of the drivers would be prepared to get her to the court. One was and she duly arrived at the door of the court in her unusual form of transport without turning a hair.

Those were the days when you could choose your own pupils. Over the years things became much more formalised. There was a chambers pupillage committee and they told you which pupil you were going to get.

I liked my women pupils but they had one disadvantage. If you were taking a load of books with you to court you had to share the burden. Young men were much more able to carry them all.

I'd had a few girls in succession and told the chair of the committee that, this time, I would prefer a man. He duly promised that he would find me one. A week or so later he invited me out to lunch, not sufficiently unusual to make me suspicious.

Seated in a small, discreet and expensive restaurant in the vicinity of the Royal Courts of Justice, surrounded by lawyers and businessmen talking in the hushed voices appropriate to the venue, Bernard poured me a glass of wine and broke it to me that my next pupil was to be a woman.

'Bernard, you *promised me.* I haven't had a man in ages!' I protested, certainly in louder tones than I had realised.

But then I saw his scarlet face. The murmured conversations around us had come to an abrupt halt. The other diners were gazing at us in undisguised fascination. The fact that I was obviously old enough to be his mother added to their interest.

Served him right.

- CHAPTER EIGHTEEN - HOW THEY ALL GREW

While I was settling very happily into my new career, the family were growing up and finding their feet in the world. One day, I hope, each of them will follow my lead and write their individual stories for themselves, their children and grandchildren.

John and I encouraged them to take up little jobs for pocket money as they reached an age where it was safe for them to do so.

Hugh began by delivering newspapers for the local newsagent, a long-suffering friend of ours. When the children were all young, each had a very small amount of weekly pocket money from us, certainly insufficient to deter them from activities which involved earning a bit more.

The newsagent was inevitably the recipient of the pocket money from home. He would wait patiently while Nora, who was very particular, would pore over his tray of sweets offered at four for a penny, select a few, change her mind and select others, and then change her mind again three or four times before making a final decision.

Hugh's appointment as paper boy was very exciting for all his brothers and sisters, although his poor employer must have rued the day when he offered him the job. Hugh's trouble was that he was quite unable to get up regularly in time for the morning delivery. Our phone would ring at about ten past six. Hugh had failed to put in an appearance once again. John would get himself out of bed, rouse Hugh and drive him to the shop. Depending on how late he was, it was sometimes John who delivered the papers by escorting Hugh around in his car.

But Hugh never got the sack, proof of the kindness of his employer. Tom took over the paper round in due course and the newsagent must have had a pleasant surprise because Tom took his duties very seriously, and was not in the habit of sleeping through the alarm clock in the morning.

At the time we had a much loved springer spaniel. Tom was fond of all animals and particularly of Lucy, who used to follow him on his round and was usually content to be left at a gate while Tom went up someone's drive to deliver the paper.

On one occasion, however, the property was surrounded by a high fence which meant that Tom had vanished from Lucy's sight.

Springers, as their name suggests, are able to jump high, so Lucy gathered herself in preparation for a vault over the fence to find him. Unfortunately, the property had a swimming pool on the other side of Lucy's chosen spot. Lucy landed in it with an enormous splash. The irate resident appeared at his front door in his pyjamas and what he said about Lucy, as he fished her out, was not complimentary.

That dog was quite a character and, we came to realise, well-known in the neighbourhood: no matter how hard we tried to keep her within the bounds of our own garden, she always found a way to get out and go for a wander. She became a particular friend of our milkman, and would sit beside him proudly at the front of his delivery cart whenever she got the chance.

It was not unusual either to get a call from the local police station: 'We've got Lucy here again, can you come and collect her?'

There she would be when we arrived, popular and petted by all the officers. I doubt whether the police would have the time or the inclination to behave like that nowadays. We would probably be facing the threat of an order to put her down.

Lucy had been preceded by Grouse, another springer, who was a gift to the children from John's brother Father Bobby, a parish priest in Limerick. Grouse was highly intelligent, and won my heart effortlessly on the day when the twins, then three years old, had between them up-ended the large family pram where Alice had been put for a sleep in the garden.

I was in the kitchen preparing a meal. Grouse came in to me barking furiously. I had no idea why, but followed him into the garden to find Alice suspended in mid air, the pram balanced precariously on its handle, only its built-in reins thankfully preventing her from falling straight out of it. Needless to say the twins had put in a disappearing act.

Unfortunately, Grouse had another side to his character. As the priest's dog, he was used to unfettered liberty to steal interesting items of food, like butcher's deliveries of fresh meat or eggs whenever he could get hold of them.

He saw no reason to change his habits just because he lived in England, and proceeded to thieve eggs left by the milkman on the doorsteps of our neighbours. He would return to us triumphant, egg all over his face, and we would have to make humiliating enquiries about where the eggs had been delivered. That resulted in many a box of chocolates or bottle of wine in compensation.

Our immediate neighbours became exasperated and no wonder – we were pretty exasperated ourselves. So back to Ireland and Father Bobby's housekeeper he had to go. She was a good soul, cooked marvellous meals for us all and loved to spoil the children when we took them over for holidays on uncle's farm, but the housekeeper's language was not quite what you might expect in a parish priest's household. Bobby would always have two or three dogs around and she would continually refer to 'them fecking dogs', an expression which I was devoutly thankful that the children failed to pick up.

In those days the priests' housekeepers ran the parishes, rather than their employers. What they said went. I remember John and I went shopping locally to buy a couple of much-needed new shirts for Bobby. His housekeeper instructed me to go to the local drapers and 'be sure to tell him that we don't need the [detachable] collars', because of course Bobby would be wearing his priestly collar, 'AND', she admonished, 'be sure he gives you a discount for that.'

Not daring to disobey, I did as she had asked. The draper sighed resignedly and remarked, 'That'll be the housekeeper then.'

Everybody knew everyone else's business in that

village. When we first arrived in our car, we asked a passer-by for directions to Bobby's house. 'Oh ye'll be the brother and his wife from England,' we were told.

No one cared to disagree with a priest. Bobby was driving us somewhere in his car and wound down the window to ask someone, 'Is this the road to...?

'Sure now, it is, Father... but you'd be quicker if you turned round.'

Another time we were in his car in Killarney driving on a country road above the famous lakes. Bobby was a disciple of the same driving school as my one-time pupil Christina, the ex-nun. He liked to progress with his head over his shoulder chatting to whoever was in the back seat. But this time a tourist ahead of us braked a little too suddenly and Bobby went into the back of her car.

It was only a small bump and Bobby immediately offered to pay for the repair. 'No! No! No!' shrieked the very irate German lady, 'We MUST call the police.'

Nothing for it but to wait until a puffed-out elderly garda arrived on his bicycle.

Civilly, he invited the lady to describe what had happened; her English was good enough to provide a graphic account of Bobby's inadequate driving skills, to the accompaniment of many impressive gestures to emphasise his iniquity.

Thanking her, the officer turned to Bobby and said, 'And what really happened, Father?'

Grouse had been Bobby's gun dog when he went out shooting rabbits, a sport for which John never had the stomach. His mouth was so gentle that when a baby bird had fallen from its nest into our garden he would bring it to us totally unharmed.

John always had a soft spot for working dogs: as a child his best friend had been the farm sheepdog. At the age of two he had fallen into a stream on the farmland and the sheepdog had grabbed his friend by the collar with its teeth and pulled him out, rescuing him from a watery grave.

One of the saddest days of his life was when that sheepdog, for some unaccountable reason, behaved totally out of character and worried one of his father's sheep. His father shot the dog. I suppose he had no alternative, but the incident left its mark on poor John, already motherless.

When we had decided that Grouse really had to be returned to Ireland the problem was how to get him there. We rang Heathrow Airport and enquired whether it would be possible to hire a cage in order to transport him to his destination. We were assured that such a hire was possible. When we named the airport the story changed.

'I'm afraid we never hire cages to Irish airports.'

'Why ever not?'

'We never get them back.'

So, no alternative to purchasing a cage at some expense. Sadly, we bid goodbye to Grouse. The children of course were heartbroken and we had to replace him, initially with a dachshund puppy called Mitzi. We had no intention of breeding from her so asked the advice of Uncle Willie, a Professor at the Veterinary College in Ireland, who specialised in the care of race horses.

He advised John about a drug used in connection with mares, but unfortunately got the dosage calculation wrong which resulted in poor Mitzi losing a lot of her hair and tending to obesity. Never mind, the children loved her, particularly Tom, as usual. Like all brothers, Hugh and Tom had their squabbles. Tom used to chant, 'Hugh without the H is Ugh!' until I put a stop to it by telling him "Tommy without the T is 'Ommy!"'

Mitzi eventually became unwell. She was lying in the garden and Mary Rose, returning from Brownies in her uniform, took out some water for her. Mitzi took a sip, rolled over and died.

'Mummy, I've killed Mitzi,' sobbed Mary Rose, but I managed to convince her that she hadn't.

A family council was held and it was decided that Mitzi would be buried in our rose bed. As we proceeded with the arrangements, Hugh made us stop. Tom was out with his scout group. 'Mummy, we can't bury Mitzi without Tom being here,' he reminded me.

I was so touched by his consideration for Tom – maybe the boys were closer than I had imagined. They are certainly close friends as adults, although still inclined to tease one another, especially about politics. I have had to ban any discussion between them on the subject of Brexit in my presence, since they hold diametrically opposed views and are not slow to give voice to them.

Much later that evening, when it was almost dark, Mary Rose had disappeared and I went to find her. She was standing, still in her Brownie uniform, by the new grave. 'I'm just saying a little prayer for Mitzi,' she explained.

It was after Mitzi that we acquired Lucy as a

puppy. She lived for seventeen years, my dog until John retired and then very much his dog. Looking back, we did allow her to get away with too much bad behaviour when she was young, but she was a faithful friend, calmed down to more acceptable conduct in the end, and is still sorely missed.

One summer holiday, Hugh found himself a temporary job with a building firm. He was a little daunted when he realised that the building he was to work on was actually just across the road from us. When his fellow builders first asked him where he lived he was deliberately vague, but in the end they found out and would tease him mercilessly about it.

Never a good time-keeper, when he was late for work having over-slept, they would summon him by calling 'Time to get up, Hugh!'

Even he found that so embarrassing that he was persuaded to turn up on time.

Tom found a holiday job as a telephone operator with British Rail, answering enquiries about the timetable. One day, by an incredible coincidence, my great friend Anne Toal rang him for help. Recognising her immediately from her distinctive Irish accent, Tom responded by calling her 'Auntie Anne'. She was so surprised she nearly dropped the phone.

At the time Tom was waiting to start training as a dentist at University College and hoping to build up some savings. Crossing the busy High Street in Bromley, he tripped when his foot was caught in a gap between the cobbles on a refuge in the middle of the road, pitched forward and was knocked down by a car. Luckily it happened on a Saturday and the traffic was crawling.

When the police arrived at Larkfield I was out shopping. John was gardening. They told him Tom had had an accident and was still unconscious. John made for the hospital, not knowing what he might find. As he arrived at Tom's bedside Tom opened his eyes and asked, 'Has anyone seen my wallet?'

'I realised then that he was going to be OK,' John told me with considerable relief.

But that was the start of months of hospitalisation for Tom, as his leg had been broken. Initially it had been badly set so he had to have the operation all over again. When we visited, he kept telling us that he had caught his foot in some obstacle. To tell the truth, at first we were too worried about him to bother with that. However, he persisted and asked me to go and look at the refuge. Six weeks after the accident I did so and indeed there was the depression he had described.

So I returned with the tape measure from my sewing bag and measured and photographed the obstacle. We wrote to our local council and suggested that some compensation might be in order. Next time I went to look, the gap had been filled with cement, but there was no reply from the council.

It was so unfair that Tom had been deprived of his chance to save for his dental course that I discussed the problem with a friend in chambers. He advised suing the council, as they would probably settle the case with an offer of money. We issued proceedings, the council denied liability and we ended up in court.

The barrister representing the council informed my barrister that he had two witnesses who would prove

Tom's case was an invention. Obviously I was going to be the principal witness in the case, so I was duly sworn and absolutely terrified. Asked my occupation I had to admit that I was a practitioner. I then described what had occurred and was, of course, vigorously cross-examined about the fact that I had not visited the scene of the accident until six weeks after it happened, and that I had used a cloth tape measure instead of a metal one.

The council's two witnesses were called. Their evidence was that they had been on the refuge when the accident took place. Tom had hurtled past them and fallen into the traffic; this of course was only confirming Tom's account.

When making his submission the council's barrister mishandled it badly. He described me as having 'gone on a fishing expedition' and ridiculed the tape measure I had used. The judge hearing the case was not at all pleased.

'The plaintiff's mother, who is a barrister of this court, has given evidence which I entirely accept,' he began. 'Furthermore I accept that the measurements she took were accurate and that those were the measurements of the obstacle on the date of the accident six weeks previously.'

So Tom won his case and was awarded over two thousand pounds which was probably more than he could have saved over the period of his incapacity. But I was devoutly hoping that never again would I find myself in the witness box!

Tom did qualify as a dentist. Hugh, after a few false starts, found his true vocation in IT, a comparatively new career at the time. My mother warned me solemnly that all IT personnel were 'burned out' by the age of thirty. Don't know where she got that idea, but he is still very happily a systems analyser, whatever that means, in his mid-sixties.

The girls also found ways to earn extra pocket money in their teens. Babysitting, looking after young children when their parents went out for an evening, was a popular and not usually too demanding pastime. Maureen was keen to start as a babysitter when John and I thought she was too young to be taking on such a responsibility. When we turned down her first offer she was incandescent: '*You,*' she accused, 'are the *worst mother* in my class!'

However, telephones were attached to walls in those days. The extension to ours was in my bedroom. As I passed the door, not knowing that she was on the phone to a friend, I heard her say proudly, 'No, my parents are very careful about me. They won't let me babysit yet because they think it's too much responsibility at my age.'

The girls all went through the babysitting stage and then graduated to waitressing in various local restaurants. Generally the pay was pretty poor, and they were expected to work for long hours but, as John would tell them, it gave them an idea of what someone, less fortunate than they were and without any qualifications, might have to be content with as a career.

It also taught them some very hard lessons about the way an employee can be treated. Mary Rose once forgot to charge a table for a bottle of expensive wine; the restaurant owner deducted the menu price, not just the wholesale price, from her meagre earnings.

But there were happier episodes; some employers would drive them home or even hire a taxi for one of them if they were working late and John, for some reason, was unable to collect them.

Most of the money the girls earned was spent on clothes, of course. I found it really touching that, if one of them had been asked to a party and another had a new dress, it would unhesitatingly be loaned for the occasion. With only one sister, Oonagh and I never swapped clothes in that way.

When Maureen started having boyfriends, John would love to call her downstairs, knowing very well that she would still be getting herself ready, and aware that I would think he was calling me. You can just imagine the horrified expressions when they saw me instead of the girl they had invited out.

Hugh and Tom still shared a bedroom – space in the house was at a premium. On one occasion there had been a local fund-raising garden party and Tom, who was in his teens, won a bottle of whiskey in a raffle. Unknown to us, he invited four of his friends to share his prize in his bedroom, with predictable results when one of them over-indulged and became violently ill. It was an accident, but unfortunately the consequences were thrown up over Hugh's bed, rather than Tom's.

We knew nothing about this until the following morning. Tom and his other friends managed to smuggle the intoxicated young man downstairs and out of the front door while we were watching something on TV. One of them had a car and was apparently sober enough to get him home: they rang his front door bell and left him on the doorstep. Hugh was far from amused when he returned, as might be expected.

When Maureen started university she found it hard to cope; a pupil at the convent until she was eighteen, she had no previous experience of mixed education and it was a big culture shock for her. After about a term she gave up and took a secretarial course – an invaluable asset throughout her life, as mine was for me. Later she returned to academia and got her degree. But her experience had taught us a lesson; the atmosphere at the convent was too rarefied: her sisters all went to sixth forms with mixed classes after that.

John had taught the boys to drive, with a little polish from professional instructors before they obtained their licences. He hoped to do the same for Maureen but found her more problematic.

Maureen always had her own ideas about how to do things. Approaching a roundabout one day, she was heading straight across, without even a glance to her right, when John had to slam his foot on the brake to prevent a serious accident. Maureen, furious, opened her door, left the car and walked home, telling him she never wanted another lesson from him!

Maureen usually had more important things on her mind when she was driving. Stopped by the police one day, she was asked if she had been drinking. She denied it indignantly.

'Nobody drives like that when they're sober,' the officer remarked. But she was.

Some years later she found a good job in advertising; a company car was included in the employment contract. She went to collect it in London and boasted triumphantly on her return that she had 'only hit two other cars' on the way back.

I hasten to add that she is a very good driver now, in Australia, where she has had her own very successful business for a number of years.

Alice decided to read law at Brunel University. She and her future husband Pat met while they were studying there. Students always found holiday jobs if they could and one of the young men in her year took up temporary employment as an outdoor clerk for a firm of solicitors, who happened to instruct me in a case and sent him along to court with the papers.

Waiting for the case to be called, we got into conversation and he told me that he was at Brunel studying law. When I realised that he was in the same year I said, 'But you must know my daughter Alice!'

He couldn't think of anyone called Alice in his year. I told him that she had a boyfriend called Pat who was a footballer. Light dawned: 'Oh, you mean *"Alice-and-Pat"?'*

They were the first couple to get married, shortly after both had qualified, Pat as a civil engineer. Alice went on to train as an accountant and became a senior government auditor with the National Audit Office. As the first son-in-law, Pat still likes to claim that he is '*numero uno*' in my affections, but he has a lot of competition. Katie's husband Adrian designed a 'Brownie Points' son-in-law chart for my ninetieth birthday; surprise, surprise, he himself turned out to be the winner!

All four of my sons-in-law are devoted husbands and fathers who care about me and make me laugh; it would be impossible to 'put a pin between them', as Granny would have said.

I have been similarly blessed with my two daughters-in-law and my thirteen grandchildren. Life without John would have been intolerable without them all.

Katie took a secretarial course and found several interesting jobs. Her last employment was with one of the firms who were pioneering office computers; her job was to go to offices which were installing the computers and train the staff who would be using them. When she discovered that her firm were charging several hundred pounds a day for this service, Katie and a friend also employed by the company decided to set up a business as independent trainers.

They had a fantastic first year but unfortunately it had not occurred to either of them that they needed to keep books for the taxman. An expensive accountant managed to sort them out, but the experience had daunted them. In any case, Katie and Adrian were about to get married. Having taken out a mortgage on a tiny modern property, Katie was able to sell it at a profit because they had decided to set up home in Tunbridge Wells.

The first home they invested in was in a bad state. Katie, always artistic and good at finding the various tradesmen needed to refurbish property, did it up and sold it at a profit.

She continued to buy run-down properties and do

them up for sale until she found a large house which had been divided into two flats; even the staircase had been removed. She spotted that the flats were being advertised for sale by two different estate agents and bought the two.

John and I took a bottle of champagne over to view their acquisition and we raised a glass to what John hoped would now be a permanent home. Adrian raised his eyes to heaven – 'It'll be Buckingham Palace next!'

First thing was to restore the staircase. Alice's husband Pat was able to perform the miracle. As usual, Katie and her band of faithful tradesmen transformed the property into a beautiful home. It was sold when the children were coming up to secondary school age; the house they purchased then was to be their home for several years.

When Katie had brought it up to her standard she had time on her hands. Mummy and Mike had been partners in a silver business in St Christopher's Place, behind Selfridges in London.

Every holiday my mother's grandchildren would take turns to help in the shop. Katie had loved the silver and learning all about the hall marks. So, all those years later, she took a course in silversmithing and now has her own successful business designing hallmarked jewellery.

Nora read Law at King's College in London and qualified as a barrister. She obtained pupillage in a very good set of chambers in Middle Temple; she was given two pupillages in the same set – a rare privilege – and started to go to court in her second six months, as is the custom. On the clerks' grapevine, I heard that she was to be offered a tenancy.

But Nora found practice was not for her. 'I'm always frightened before I go into court,' she told me. Unpersuaded by my assurances that every barrister starts off like that, she chose to continue her studies for a master's degree at Trinity College Cambridge, where she obtained first-class honours. Still finding a career at the bar unattractive, she re-qualified as a solicitor.

She is now a media lawyer specialising in music contracts. Glamorous and beautifully dressed, she is a much-loved role model for her nieces; she is kind, generous to a fault, always interested in what they and her nephews are doing, encouraging them and advising them.

I am so fortunate that she lives in London. We meet up frequently, share our troubles and our joys, go to the theatre, concerts and the cinema, have meals out and laugh a lot. Not so easy under lockdown, but we still manage socially distanced get-togethers.

Mary Rose qualified as a solicitor and practised in London at first. James, now her husband, met her before John died. John liked him from the start – we all did – but solemnly warned me, 'He'll never marry Mary – he's a typical Irish bachelor', an exact repetition of what my father always used to say about him!

He would have so loved to see himself proved wrong, but that was not to be. James and Mary Rose married two years after we lost him. This meant, of course, that their daughter Rosie was the only grandchild not to have known John, although when she was little she used to claim that she had met him in heaven before she was born. And who are we to say she didn't?

When Mary Rose was in primary school she was taking part in an elocution contest. Her poem was about a rabbit caught in a snare. I can still vividly recall the beginning and the end: 'I hear a sudden cry of pain … little one, oh little one, I am searching *everywhere*.'

What made her delivery so compelling was that you knew that her compassion for the poor creature was completely genuine. Mary Rose felt for anyone who was in trouble and it came across.

When she had qualified as a solicitor she gave up some of her spare time to give free legal advice at a local centre. Her proudest possession was a battered little yellow motor car which she had acquired second-hand. One night she left the centre to find that it had been completely vandalised. 'Probably,' she admitted sadly, 'by one of the people I had been advising.'

But that didn't stop her wanting to help the disadvantaged.

- CHAPTER NINETEEN - GOLF AND FRIENDS

Daddy had always loved playing golf and made determined attempts to introduce me to its mysteries when I was a teenager. Unfortunately, I never took to it at that stage. Ridiculously self-conscious, if there was another player within my vision, I would be convinced that he or she would be observing my pitiful efforts with disdain, at that stage unaware of the eternal truth that the only thing any golfer on a course is interested in is his or her own performance.

I had never envisaged becoming a member of a golf club, having written myself off from a sporting viewpoint on the gym teacher's pronouncement that I was 'the blot on her horizon' – a lay member of staff, of course, not one of the lovely nuns.

I was expecting Alice when John met Dick Buckley and brought him home to meet me. Dick explained to me that his wife Nan was about to give birth to their second baby and we would meet when the baby had arrived safely. But I saw him, with Nan, at Mass the following Sunday and said to John, with conviction, 'She isn't even pregnant!'

Lucky Nan never seemed to show a pregnancy unlike me. I was already huge and Alice wasn't due for a few months. Nan's cleaner was so shocked when Dick told her about the arrival of one of their babies that she excused herself and asked if she could sit down. 'I had no idea she was expecting,' she explained.

Nan and Dick were to become our closest friends, living round the corner from us, with their – eventually – six children and our seven. Although Bridget and my third child Alice were some months apart, there were only three weeks between their Nuala and our Katie, ten days between their Richard and our Nora.

The four of us had escaped to Paris for a weekend early on in that pregnancy. A French saleswoman had been rude to me – I couldn't stop my stupid tears. When they got back to their hotel room, Nan said to Dick, 'Maureen's pregnant too.'

We had other close friends in the area. On our first day at Mass in St Joseph's, our parish in Bromley, John was astounded to notice Ivor Morris seated a couple of benches ahead of us. They had gone through medical school in Dublin together, seated beside one another for lectures because the seating was in alphabetical order. Ivor and his lovely wife Gwen made us welcome to the area and were also friends of Nan and Dick.

We all loved driving down into Kent to local pubs which served good meals. Once, in Westerham, four couples expecting babies were ranged round a tea table. A rather camp young waiter brought the tea pot and enquired, 'Who's going to be mother then?'

Poor man, he really suffered when we all laughed.

John and Dick had become members of Sundridge Park Golf Club and plotted together that Nan and I should join too. Nan was much more sporting that I but the other three managed to persuade me to take it up and I never regretted it, although never acquired any handicap under twenty-seven while John clung to his twenty-four.

Mary and Jim MacNamara were close friends too, also golfers. Their house overlooked the first green which meant that Jim's dog was able to keep us supplied with lost balls. Mary and I were playing one day when the dog escaped from their garden and, barking joyously in recognition of his mistress, joined us on the green. An irate member who was taking his golf seriously approached us and angrily enquired whether the dog belonged to either of us. 'Never seen him before in my life,' Mary assured him, without batting an eyelid, while the dog jumped all over her, wagging its tail furiously.

Bill McConnell went to a wedding in Ireland, met Joan there and brought her back to Bromley as an incredibly young bride a year later. My daughter Nora, friends with her daughter Siobhan, loved visiting their home, shared with Bill's mother who came from Scotland herself and lived to be ninety-nine years old. That redoubtable lady always enjoyed a party and there were many parties at her address. At one of these I was chatting with her and noticed that her glass was empty. 'Would it be all right to give Granny a second whiskey?' I asked Joan.

'She's had three already, but who's counting?' her daughter-in-law replied.

Throughout her ninety-ninth year Bill's mother was planning her hundredth birthday party. Joan was keeping the names for the guest list but it was no easy task. 'You know the woman. We see her at Mass,' Granny would announce, 'I invited her to my party.'

Poor Joan would have no idea who she was talking about.

It has to be admitted that Granny preferred the company of men to women. Bishop Charles was visiting the parish and it was announced that he was coming to see Granny. 'You must do my hair,' Granny instructed, 'and advise me about what I should wear.'

As I have already mentioned, we had the pleasure of welcoming several *au pair* girls into the family over the years. Many remained friends; some have passed away. Pilar, Teresa and Nuria all came from Barcelona. John and I called in there on one of our cruises and the three girls, who had not previously met one another, were lined up to meet us at the port. They showed us around their beautiful city and we had a wonderful lunch together.

A couple of years ago I visited Barcelona again with Alice, Pat and Nora. Pilar and Teresa were there to give us a great welcome.

All the men belonged to a Catholic association called the Catenians. Their unofficial motto is 'Faith, Family, Friends and Fun.'

It was certainly a valued support to us as growing young Catholic families and we made lifelong friends in the association. I met Kathleen, one of my dearest friends still, at a Catenian dance in London when we were both eighteen, born only days apart. She later became a much-loved member of the family when she joined Mummy and Michael to help in their shop in St Christopher's Place.

It is my proud boast that my paternal grandfather, Charlie McAleer, was one of the founders of the Catenians in Glasgow where the second circle was opened. My father followed his example. My John, Oonagh's John and my brothers Jimmy and Michael were also members. So my sons, Hugh and Tom, were the fourth generation in the family to become members, a record unequalled in the association, as far as I know.

When Daddy was president of his Catenian circle it held a dinner at the Mansion House. We were all invited of course. Hugh, then about sixteen, attended his first formal occasion in a hired dinner jacket.

The Catenians held an annual golf week in the spring, visiting some of the best courses in the British Isles and the Republic of Ireland. They were such happy holidays, meeting up with so many friends. A couple of them were held in Waterville, County Kerry. One of our party booked a lesson from the pro at the club. At the end of the lesson he asked how much he owed his instructor, 'Ah, sure I couldn't charge you anything,' was the slightly disconcerting response. 'I haven't been able to improve you at all.'

We had a widowed friend who had not played for a long time. We managed to persuade him to accompany us on one of the golf tours. We were in a Stableford match, where individual players score points. An average score would be in the high twenties or the thirties, a total in the forties will win.

My friend was on the last green. I had finished and asked him his score as we walked to the clubhouse. 'I got three,' he told me

'George, what happened?'

'Well,' he explained, 'I got three on the first nine, and in the second nine I really began to go to pieces.'

Rather surprisingly, in view of our low handicaps, both John and I managed to get a hole in one; many much more accomplished players do not share that distinction, since a lot of luck comes into the achievement, particularly at our level.

John's was the first. He was representing Bromley circle against Upminster circle in a singles match. His opponent happened to be John Keefe. The last hole on the Essex course has a short downhill approach with the difficulty that the green is invisible from the tee.

Theirs was the final match in the competition. As it happened the scores were all square so the teams who had finished were having a drink outside the clubhouse overlooking the final green eagerly anticipating the result from the two Johns.

He drove off and heard a cheer from the assembled spectators, assuming glumly that he had played such a bad shot that they were mocking him. He would not believe that his ball was in the hole until he had had a look.

Wives had been invited to the dinner afterwards. Oonagh had arranged to pick me up at Upminster station so that I could change from my court clothes into my glad rags. When we got back to her house we found John Keefe's clubs in the hall. We didn't know what to think until we found his note on the kitchen table: 'Mullally got a hole in one. Came back for cheque book.'

I still have that note. And the drawing our eldest grandson John made of Grandpa on that happy occasion – with his hair sticking straight up in the air as it often did when he was outdoors. John was only five but children can be disconcertingly observant.

My own hole in one was a few years later in Portugal and was a complete fluke, but then I suppose most of them are.

When I was about fifty, I was cornered one day by Canon Joe and another priest friend. They had decided to nominate me for membership of the Knights of the Holy Sepulchre, an organisation dedicated to the support of the few remaining Christians in the Holy Land. I had barely heard of the KHS and wondered why they should think of me.

They were brutally frank: 'It's John we really want, but we know that he will only come in if you are invested first.'

How well they knew him. He was invested a couple of years later. We gained so many dear friends in the Order and made several pilgrimages over the years to visit parishes, schools, the seminary and university in Bethlehem, together with the holy places associated with the life of Christ, for all of which we had pledged our prayers and financial support. Above all, we were able to meet the people, so courageous and hospitable, insistent on inviting us to meals when most of them had so little to live on.

After John had left us I continued to go on pilgrimage until I became physically too frail to be anything but a burden to others taking part. Back in the United Kingdom there are still days of recollection, Masses and other KHS functions which I can attend. My dear friend Joan McConnell is the president of my section in Southwark; now that I live in London I attend Westminster section events too.

- CHAPTER TWENTY -
MORE ABOUT THE BAR

The relationship of a barrister with his/her clerk is crucial to a successful practice. It was Stanley who took the decisions when a barrister like me was starting off. He kept a watchful eye on my progress and it was he who gradually directed my career, judging when I was ready to take on more difficult work and taking full responsibility for advising solicitors that I would be able to cope with more complicated cases. It was sad when he left chambers, even sadder when his first successor was a man who disliked me from the outset and made his dislike quite evident. Whether this was just about me or whether he had a problem with women, which I suspected was the case, it made for a miserable couple of years.

Fortunately, he left after a reasonably short time and was succeeded by Gary, still chief clerk in chambers and a very good friend to this day.

One of the supreme advantages of the clerking system is that barristers never have any problem about fixing fees – all that is done by the clerk, generally without any consultation with the individual barrister; at least this was true in my case. I relied on Stanley and his successors in the job completely.

This came in very handy on an occasion when I was

being instructed to represent a Catholic newspaper in a dispute with one of its employees. The solicitor had the impudence to suggest to Stanley that, in view of my own faith, I might be prepared to take the case on a 'pro bono' basis – in other words for no fee.

Stanley, himself a Catholic, had no hesitation in making an appropriate response: 'Chambers,' he informed the offending solicitor with dignity, 'have no intention of accepting fifteen percent of Mrs Mullally's reward in heaven.'

John only agreed to come to see me in court on one occasion, shortly before my retirement. He said he had one idea of me and did not want it changed. I think he had watched too many American detective TV dramas and imagined that I would be shouting and browbeating people as the lawyers in those programmes always seemed to be doing.

As a matter of fact, I consciously modelled myself on my first pupil master, Margaret Booth, who was invariably calm and courteous in her approach to witnesses, her opponents in cases and any tribunal where she was appearing. But she got results!

One barrister who had been against me in a case met another member of my chambers and warned him not be deceived by that 'mild manner' of mine. 'When you get inside the court,' he added, 'it's like being shot in the back of the knees by the IRA!'

Well, I had won the case, but not by being in the least bit belligerent.

A couple of American law students shadowed me for a few days once; they simply could not get over the politeness of members of the English bar to one another. In the United States, they told me, lawyers were invariably rude to their opponents both inside and outside court. Their clients expected them to be and would have been disappointed otherwise.

In our courts it was – and I hope still is – the custom that you referred to your opposite number as 'my learned friend'. I was cross examining a witness about an answer she had given to her barrister when she had been examined in chief: 'You told my learned friend…' I began. She stopped me in my tracks. '*I* don't know who your friend is!'

The judge had to hide a smile.

The first time I accompanied Margaret to the Court of Appeal she asked me to go back to chambers to pick up some authorities – cases reported in the Law Reports which she wanted to rely on in support of her appeal. The volumes containing the reports are extremely heavy. As it was my first time in the court room I had no idea that there were steps I had to climb to reach the silks' row and couldn't see them over the books.

Reports and I crashed to the ground with a thunderous clamour which stopped Margaret's submissions in full flow. Worse yet, the three appeal judges burst out laughing at my predicament. It was one of the newspaper reporters who helped me pick them up and whispered consolingly, 'Everyone does that their first time.'

Somehow, I doubted that.

However, there was one occasion when the authorities came to my rescue. With my final submission in a case only part made, I realised that my judge had actually fallen asleep – too much wine at lunch perhaps?

What to do? Inspiration came and I gave the pile of the books in front of me a sharp elbowing which caused them to cascade to the floor with considerable clatter.

The judge came to with a start and I finished my clearly less than compelling submission with his complete attention.

A friend of mine had been appearing in the court of appeal and happened to run into one of the judges hearing his case at a social function later that evening. 'I had the pleasure of appearing before you this afternoon,' my friend reminded him, devastatingly as it turned out. 'Yes, indeed,' was the courteous reply, 'and when I was listening to your submissions I lost the will to live.'

Judges became less terrifying when one learned that they made human errors like the rest of us. One much-loved member of the court of appeal was convicted of driving with an excess of alcohol in his blood when police local to his home intercepted him between the railway station and his address after a dinner at his inn of court. A criminal conviction, of course. His friends in the legal profession, of whom there were many, feared that his role as an appeal court judge might have to come to a summary end. Not a bit of it. The powers that be decided that he could continue in his appointment, with the proviso that he should not be part of any tribunal trying a case in which alcohol was involved.

Dame Rose Heilbron, the second woman to be appointed a high court judge, was never keen on alcoholic excess. I was representing a gentleman against whom his wife was making several complaints in the hope of getting him removed from the matrimonial home; one of her allegations was that he drank too much.

When we all returned to her court after the luncheon adjournment, the judge began to sniff suspiciously. 'Mrs Mullally, do you detect the smell of alcohol?'

That enquiry was a bit of a poser for me. I thought I could smell alcohol, but I was pretty sure that it was coming from my instructing solicitor who was sitting behind me. I replied, 'I'm not sure, my lady,' which was the simple truth.

John had always been the decision maker in our relationship. He would mull things over in his own mind until he had come to a firm conclusion and then let me know what that conclusion was. I can't see any of my daughters allowing that to happen with their husbands, but I recognised early on that this was going to be a feature of our marriage. I might argue a bit, but he invariably convinced me that he knew best – quite simply, he did.

When he was approaching seventy, we were on holiday at La Manga Club one evening dining at a favourite restaurant, when he mentioned casually that he was planning to retire in a few months.

I said immediately that I would retire too. 'Nonsense,' I was told, 'you love your career. You're still in your fifties. I'll be playing golf with Jim MacNamara every day; you'd only be getting in my way!'

So, for the next ten years I continued to practise. John would drive me to the station every day and collect me every evening. If I had a case which was going to last for a few days in Brighton or some other far-flung venue, as happened fairly often, we would book into a comfortable local country pub with a good restaurant. John would potter about exploring the area while I was in court and we would meet up for dinner.

John began to take an interest in cooking. I can still remember my delighted astonishment the first time I returned from court to the delicious smell of a steak casserole he had invented with Guinness as its base. He signed up for a cookery class near where we lived, but had to give it up when he realised that he was the only male participant – and that every widowed lady on the course seemed to have assumed he was a widower in search of a new wife.

We still kept up our habit of attending and giving dinner parties within our circle of friends. That could be pretty exhausting when combined with a full-on career. On one such occasion poor John, the host, tried to catch my eye at the other end of our table and realised, to his horror, that I had fallen asleep!

There was always something interesting going on in chambers; as a general common law set we were a mixed bunch. Men and women who have followed other careers sometimes read for the Bar in their retirement years, their former expertise in their own fields contributing not a little to their successes in court.

When the ex-headmaster of one of the public schools applied for a pupillage with us, he found himself confronted on the interviewing committee by one of his old pupils. Fortunately, they had always enjoyed a good relationship. He became a member and a successful practitioner.

So it caused no surprise when a woman colleague, who specialised in medical negligence, decided to take on a gentleman in his late fifties, a surgeon who had had enough, he told us of the NHS and the way it was run, took early retirement and went to Bar School.

He was completely charming and very anxious to help in any way he could. I tripped and fell on our stone staircase wrenching my knee badly; he was kindness itself, examining my leg with professional gentleness and happy to assure me that I hadn't broken anything. My mother was critically ill in hospital; he offered to have a word with her medical team for me.

High court judges sometimes invite people with specialised knowledge to sit on the bench when they are hearing cases related to their particular area of expertise. My colleague had a friend trying a case of medical negligence in the Royal Courts of Justice and arranged that her pupil should receive an invitation to sit with the judge.

Members of chambers have meetings for the purpose of deciding whether a pupil should be offered a tenancy. Before this gentleman had even embarked on his second pupillage with us, we had all agreed that he would be a welcome addition to our numbers.

Pupils start going to court in their second six months; our solicitors were completely bowled over by his charm and authoritative presence, as were their clients. He was quite obviously on the brink of a great triumph in his new vocation. Then came the shock. The cases he had been appearing in had been funded by Legal Aid. The Legal Aid Board had contacted our clerks to tell them that they had been unable to find his name on the Bar List.

It turned out that he had not been called to the Bar, nor had he attended Bar school. How silly that no one had checked, but in those days you just couldn't imagine anyone practising that kind of deceit.

We never saw him again, once the clerks had contacted him. But we did discover that, under another name, he had actually been employed as a surgeon for several years – again, without bothering to take any exams!

I came in for a fair amount of teasing about my knee, of course.

- CHAPTER TWENTY-ONE - NOT MEETING ANTHONY HOPKINS AND OTHER BRUSHES WITH CELEBRITY

No doubt about it, my friends John, Tony and I shared one of the most gorgeous rooms in historic Middle Temple, situated on a corner of the first floor of the building, just inside and to the left of the Embankment entrance to Middle Temple Lane. Our bow windows looked over the garden and down to the River Thames. The room itself was spacious and our furnishings comfortable. I owned a magnificent antique 'partners' desk of which I was inordinately proud. We were situated in an 'annexe' to the main chambers building, Lamb Building, which did not enjoy the same views, so we counted ourselves particularly fortunate.

Another colleague in chambers had a sister-in-law in the film business. She was involved in a forthcoming production which included a scene where there was to be a conference with a barrister, and asked me if she could bring her producer to look at my room, to give him an idea of an authentic venue.

Along they came and inspected our room. A couple

of days later this girl phoned and asked if it would be possible to use my room for the scene. The plot was concerned with an acrimonious divorce, coincidentally enough, and Anthony Hopkins was playing the part of a father trying to obtain custody of his child.

I laughed at the idea and explained that she would have to obtain the permission of Middle Temple and my head of chambers, which I thought would probably be impossible. 'Don't worry about that,' she assured me. 'I've already discussed it with both and have their permission.'

She then explained that there would be no fee payable by the film company. However, they were going to re-decorate the room, install additional bookcases and provide me with a case of champagne as compensation for their being able to take it over for one day of filming.

Not only that, I would be meeting Anthony Hopkins, playing the part of the father. He only happened to be my favourite actor at the time!

It didn't take me long to agree, obviously with the consent of Tony and John, and a date was fixed.

Before that day arrived I had a case away from London which was to last a couple of weeks. On my return to chambers I reminded my chief clerk of the agreed date for the filming. 'Well no,' he said sadly. 'It's not happening after all.'

I was so disappointed, especially about Anthony Hopkins. 'What on earth…'

The film company wanted to know what the penalty would be if they over-ran the two days.

In my absence they had approached my head of

chambers. He had said that an over-run would cost them £400 a day – unsurprisingly they had found another venue in a rival set of chambers – with nothing like our view!

So no re-decoration, no additional shelving, no champagne – and no meeting with my favourite actor.

But I did have other brushes with celebrity, in addition to the encounter with Margaret Thatcher already described. I met various members of the royal family too. There are four Inns of Court, every barrister is called to the Bar in one of them: Middle Temple, Inner Temple, Lincoln's Inn and Gray's, where I had been called. It is a tradition that each Inn has a royal patron. When I was eating my dinners, then an essential prerequisite to a career at the Bar, Prince Charles was patron of Gray's, and visited regularly.

I had booked a place for dinner on a night when he was due to be with us. He had only been married to Princess Diana for a few months at the time. As everyone must know, punctuality is an abiding virtue with our royal family, but we were in for a surprise. He did not arrive at the appointed hour. Hungry and thirsty, we stood at our places at the long tables waiting for his appearance with increasing impatience.

Eventually, decanters of sherry were distributed and we were told we could sit down. To my recollection he was at least three-quarters of an hour late. Of course there was no explanation or apology, but his flustered demeanour made some of us suspect that it might have been some kind of domestic crisis which had delayed him.

At that time women barristers were very much in

the minority. I had been hoping that he might decide to have a word with me as he progressed down the hall to the benchers' table, stopping to have a chat with people as he passed. A vain hope – there were a few young women students and he made a bee-line for them, very understandably.

When I became a member of Middle Temple it was the Queen Mother who was our patron, and immensely popular she was. On her death, she was replaced by Princess Diana. I had booked for her first dinner with us and was really looking forward to meeting her. Photographs simply did not do her justice. She was one of the most beautiful women I had ever seen, wearing a simple gown in midnight blue which accentuated the colour of her amazing eyes.

Before she arrived the Treasurer, the most senior person in the Inn, had explained the correct form of address – should she speak to us we were to call her Your Royal Highness and after that Ma'am. Just before she entered the hall he rushed back to tell us that she had enquired what masters of the bench were usually called and been told 'Master'.

'Then that's what I want to be called,' she told him.

She sat in the middle of the benchers' table, of course, with the Treasurer beside her. On her other side, one of the young pupils was given the honour of a place. Unsurprisingly, he was so fascinated by her that his lamb cutlets were left untasted. 'Are you not going to eat them?' she asked.

When informed that he was not, she said, 'Well, pass them on to my plate, they are really delicious.'

After dinner we had all been divided into groups of

four to stand in our allotted places so that we could be presented to her. One of my four was the famous TV broadcaster Robin Day, feared by the mighty and powerful for his ability to skewer them with his persistent and revealing questions during his news interviews. He was as nervous as any boy in her presence, his hands actually shaking.

When her lady in waiting gently reminded her that it was time to leave, Diana refused to go. 'I'm having such a lovely time,' she protested.

So were we.

Cumberland Lodge in Windsor Great Park is a magnificent country mansion dating from the seventeenth century, with a history of famous occupants, culminating in the proprietorship of one of Queen Victoria's daughters. George VI and Queen Elizabeth, parents of our present Queen, set up a charitable foundation there where conferences and discussions are held all year round so that young people can be given the opportunity to meet and debate wide matters of social and moral interest.

My second husband, Neil Clarke, was associated with the governing body there for thirty-seven years and was instrumental in carrying out much needed refurbishment of the property, together with ensuring that its work became financially profitable for the charity. A room where board meetings take place has been dedicated to his name. It is situated between the library and the garden, reflecting Neil's favourite pursuits.

As a member of the Family Law Bar Association, I attended several weekends at Cumberland Lodge at a time when the Queen Mother was still alive, and subsequently when Elizabeth II became the patron. Those taking part were invariably invited to attend the Royal Chapel services on Sunday mornings.

On one such occasion John and I and our fellow guests were told that several members of the royal family were in attendance. They were seated behind a screen to one side of the altar so we would not be able to see them. However, at the end of the service, to my considerable surprise, the principal of Cumberland Lodge seized my wrist and breathlessly instructed me to come with him. My thought was that we might be taken to see the royals get into their cars.

Not a bit of it. Outside the chapel entrance, in a receiving line, were the Queen Mother, the Queen, Prince Philip, Prince Edward and his fiancée. We were the first out of the building. Before I knew what was happening I was being presented to the Queen Mother. I tried to execute the curtsey which Madame Vacani had instilled in us at Brentwood, but all I could think about was that, surely, a terrible mistake had been made and we ought to have been presented to the Queen first.

Later it was explained to me that the chapel belonged to the Queen Mother. I had no time to concern myself with that, however, realising that I was being asked what the purpose of our conference was. I explained that we had invited lawyers from Eire and Northern Ireland to share the experience and added, I hoped helpfully, that the gentleman following John was the president of the Eire High Court.

In the meantime, poor John had decided that the

only way to meet royalty was to genuflect as he would have done in church. The response was a charming smile and a word about his Irish ancestry and my Scottish birth – 'a perfect combination' she thought.

When the turn of the distinguished Irish lawyer came, she confided in him that she had had an exhausting week at Ascot races. 'You must be cleaned out,' he said sympathetically.

'Yes, I am,' she agreed.

The remaining introductions were effected. It was all over so quickly and we had had no warning that it would take place. Probably worked out better that way – at least no time to be nervous.

A subsequent meeting with Prince Philip was not quite so successful. I had been invited to the Queen's celebration of the fiftieth anniversary of an organisation committed to bringing together members of the Jewish and Catholic faiths. A number of the invitees were, like me, members of the Knights of the Holy Sepluchre, an Order dedicated to the support of Christians in the Holy Land, by prayer and financial contributions.

When my turn came, Prince Philip seemed to find this irritating. 'What *is* the Order of the Holy Sepulchre?' he enquired, with some disdain.

I couldn't resist the temptation, 'It's a bit like the Freemasons.'

He turned on his heel and walked away from me.

Middle Temple enjoyed a close social relationship with the Irish Bar. John had been very keen for me to be called at King's Inns in Dublin. I had to secure references from my head of chambers, my former pupil masters and the attorney general, but once all that had been done there were no further exams to be taken. A friend and I were called on the same day amid a considerable amount of celebration. The head of the Irish judiciary gave us a warm welcome from the Bench, adding that they would always be delighted to see us on social occasions, but that he hoped we were not 'planning to take the bread out of the mouths of decent Irish barristers'. Fortunately, we weren't.

Every alternate summer parties from Ireland and Middle Temple exchanged long weekends. Husbands and wives were invited, of course. Initially John and I caused some confusion because it was always assumed that he was the lawyer.

When Mary Robinson became the first woman president of Ireland she was invited to become a bencher of Middle Temple. John and I were at the dinner to celebrate the occasion. Mary's father, a GP in Ireland was there too; he and John, fellow medics in a sea of lawyers, found solace in one another's company.

The next time Middle Temple were invited to Ireland there were fewer than twenty of us. Mary invited us to visit her for drinks at the presidential residence, where she discussed her family with us and showed us the light which she kept burning every night from a window on an upper floor to welcome Irish emigrants home.

In 1993 she became the first Irish head of state to meet a British sovereign, spending a few days in London. John and I were astounded to receive an invitation to meet her from the Irish ambassador, never having been inside the embassy before. John was sure it was because of my links with the Irish Bar.

When we arrived, however, it soon became clear that he was the object of the invitation. Mary had told the ambassador that she didn't want the 'usual rent-a-crowd' on their guest list, but rather Irish men and women who had made contributions to life in Britain – priests, nuns, doctors like John and other caring professionals.

One chap who had qualified with John was definitely one of the rent-a-crowd. 'Two cats couldn't have a fight in the street without him refereeing it,' was the way John described him to me once. He happened to be just after us in the reception line. 'But I know you already!' the president exclaimed smilingly when John was presented to her. His friend was not a little taken aback. She didn't know him.

- CHAPTER TWENTY-TWO - THE HOUSE OF LORDS

When you feel the judge has got it wrong you can always, in theory at least, appeal his or her judgment. That was true, anyway, until the appeal court got so fed up with appeals from family judges that they ruled, in a never-to-be forgotten case called G v G, that the judge who had actually pronounced judgment in a dispute about a child, having heard the evidence and had an opportunity to assess the parents concerned, could only be appealed if the decision appeared to the court to be beyond the generous ambit of 'judicial discretion'.

That was in 1985. When I read the law report in *The Times* on my way to court, my heart sank, undoubtedly in unison with the hearts of the majority of my family law colleagues, but it was inevitable that it would come to pass, so much appeal court time was being taken up by family work.

Divorce was a fairly modern phenomenon when I began my legal career, to the point that John and I only knew one couple who had been divorced. Until 1969 one spouse had to be at fault – whether it be by adultery, cruelty or desertion. The Divorce Reform Act brought in two new ways to end a marriage: the couple could agree to end it after two years of separation or, if only one wanted it, five years of separation.

Until 1970 family matters had been dealt with in the Probate Divorce and Admiralty division of the High Court – colloquially known as 'wills, wives and wrecks'. I met a judge who had heard cases in that division and told me that he had never worried over which marine insurance company should pay a huge sum of money as damages, when there had been a collision between two massive cargo ships, but had spent many sleepless nights anxious about which of two good parents should have the custody of their child.

As already explained, I was initially concerned about whether I should be involved in divorce at all, but Stanislaus had explained that divorce was a purely civil law matter and did not affect the sacramental nature of the marriage. In fact, there were marriages where priests would advise members of their flocks to obtain civil divorce to free them from intolerable situations.

In those cases a practising Catholic would not be free to marry again in the church, but the church has its own courts where an annulment of a sacramental marriage may be obtained in certain circumstances. In the end I became quite an expert on the law of the Church in relation to decrees of nullity and in a position to advise clients on it when appropriate.

Shortly after the case had been reported I had an appeal against an order about a child listed. As I entered the court, the usher whispered to me, 'Haven't you heard about G v G?'

Very dispiriting. She was right of course.

When I was Margaret's pupil, divorce petitions had to be held in court – hers were all in the High Court. She could get through about eleven in a morning. My job was to take a careful note of everything that was said by the parties and, of course, the judge. My shorthand really helped there. Nowadays, there is no court hearing. It is all a matter of paperwork.

As I have already made clear, I was terrified when I had an appeal case. On one occasion I was waiting my turn outside the court when I noticed two men standing at some distance away. Returning to my papers, it struck me that there was something familiar about them. I looked again – the two men were my father and one of my sons.

Most family cases are heard 'in chambers', meaning in private, with only the parties and the lawyers present. But appeal cases are always in open court. People can come in to watch them. Daddy had decided to take the opportunity to see me in action and had brought his grandson with him.

One of the worst days I had in the appeal court was in a case called H. The parents had disputed custody. I was for the husband and the wife represented herself. The father was given custody of the two boys. The mother had appealed. Lunching in Hall a couple of days previously, counsel representing the mother had introduced himself and we chatted about the case, which was due to be listed the following day.

That evening, however, my clerks told me that the hearing had been deferred. Next day I ambled into chambers wearing casual clothes, as I planned to concentrate on paperwork. I was doing exactly that at about midday when my senior clerk arrived to inform me that the clerk to the court of appeal was on the phone asking where I was.

I shot over to the robing room and somehow contrived to arrange my robes to disguise my less than professional garb by turning a black cardigan back to front to conceal the absence of a white shirt. As I entered the court, blushing furiously, my opponent welcomed me audibly: 'Nice of you to turn up.'

He was a piece of work all right. Any other barrister I knew would have contacted my chambers when waiting for the first case to be heard and given me time to be there. He left it, knowing very well what a humiliation it would be for me.

The three judges were waiting with ill-concealed impatience. No wonder, it must have been almost unheard of for counsel to be late. 'No apologies or explanations today, Mrs Mullally. Leave all that until tomorrow.'

My opponent then launched into his appeal. The basis of his argument was that his poor client had been unrepresented and I had shamelessly taken advantage of her by including in my submission to the judge matters which had not been raised in my client's affidavit. There was no time that day for me to try to make any response.

On return to chambers Stanley was as disconsolate as I was myself. However, it turned out that there had been two cases with the same surname listed and the clerk to the court of appeal had mixed them up when speaking to Stanley. He promised he would accompany me the following day and apologise with me.

A sleepless night. But when my clerk and I went into court the three judges were all smiles. 'We have heard about the mistake and no apology is necessary.'

Furthermore,' with a glance at my opponent, 'we have had an opportunity to consider the father's affidavit and we do not accept that Mrs H was taken advantage of in any way.'

My unpleasant opponent duly lost his appeal.

In those days judgments were not recorded on tape. Where there was to be an appeal counsel had to agree a note of the judgment, to be submitted to the judge for his approval. My shorthand gave me a massive advantage here. Other members of the Bar would only have scrappy notes in their own handwriting. I would have recorded every word, and was able to send over a neatly typed transcription for agreement, which was invariably obtained, together with the judge's blessing. One grumbled, 'You even put in my hesitations… '

Chambers employed one typist, Beryl. A dozen or so members would be giving her handwritten pieces of work, waiting their turn in the queue, having to check she had interpreted their writing correctly and then waiting for any errors to be corrected. Stanislaus used to say that Beryl could correct his opinions on law if required.

I never needed Beryl's services.

Technology did come to the courts in the end. When laptops were being introduced, an expert was invited to instruct the judges of the High Court in the mysteries of their use. Some mentioned that they were experiencing problems.

'There are no problems with computers, only opportunities,' their mentor explained cheerfully.

From the back of the room a mournful voice was heard to claim, 'Well, I've found an insoluble opportunity on mine!'

Occasionally, one of my cases might win a place in the law reports, but my most brilliant achievement was the one which made the House of Lords. Only matters which clarify some point of law were heard by that august body, now replaced by the much more mundane Supreme Court, where the judges wear dreary facsimiles of the costumes worn by European judges , rather than their former magnificent robes.

My case concerned a very young child born of an unmarried couple, the mother Irish, the father Moroccan. Tragically the mother died suddenly. Her mother and an unmarried sister came to England, hi-jacked the little boy and removed him to Ireland, applying to the High Court there for an order for custody. The judge wisely refused to deal with the matter, finding that the appropriate jurisdiction was the English court.

The father was my client and we made an urgent application to the High Court for the immediate return of the boy to his father.

On the initial hearing of my application the Irish family were represented. The judge declined to make an order and adjourned the matter for hearing a few days later. On that application counsel for the Irish family announced that he had several witnesses to call and the judge found that the hearing should be postponed for lack of time.

Time is of the essence when it comes to a young child. The court's decisions will always be directed to the child's best interests. The longer the Irish family could hang on to him, the more chance they would have of keeping him permanently.

It was clear that there was going to be a battle royal about him. Counsel for the Irish family was submitting that a full hearing would take several days, which indeed it did. His principal argument was that the father had no legal standing. In those days an unmarried father, not named on the birth certificate, could get 'paternal rights' but it had to be with the mother's consent. That had never been given.

The Irish family were wealthy; a nanny had been engaged to care for the little boy. Until the case was heard it was necessary to make arrangements for his father to have 'access' to him, to be able to see him at reasonable intervals. The father was granted access in Ireland, but somewhat ironically in view of the history of the matter, the Irish family insisted that it must take place in the presence of one of the family or someone appointed by them, in case the father abducted him.

He was not at all well off, but travelled to Ireland for every access visit, to be enjoyed under supervision. The case was heard in the High Court and was appealed. Finally, an appeal to the House of Lords was granted, on the basis that the important point about whether a father in such circumstances had any right to the child had never been decided.

Unsurprisingly, all this took almost eighteen months.

In the House of Lords, both counsel were led by

silks; mine was Judith Parker, my opponent's Patricia Scotland, subsequently attorney general, currently Secretary-General of the Commonwealth of Nations.

We had a five-man tribunal, underlining the importance of the question to be resolved. I was petrified and launched the day by knocking over the carafe of water kindly provided at my elbow. A lackey in uniform rushed over with a pile of snowy napkins to clear up the mess which did not seem to be unanticipated. The judges were not in robes, which felt a little odd as we were all gowned and wigged. They reserved their judgments, curiously known as 'opinions', for some weeks.

At last the big day came. It was an even bigger day for me, because it was the first and only time that John came to court to see me in action, accompanied by our Australian son-in-law Bill. Judith was otherwise engaged so I was alone.

Oddly, we were given the opinions in the robing room before we reached the court. There were no dissenting views, all five judges found in favour of our argument that an unmarried father, not having been granted parental responsibility, was still a father, with a legitimate legal interest in his child.

It was a bitter-sweet moment because the child had now been resident with the Irish family for far too long for the tribunal to consider making an order that he be given back to his father. It was no surprise when we were told that there was to be a psychological assessment of the child's attachments to his various relatives.

What was a surprise when it came was the

conclusion of the psychologist: the little boy's closest emotional attachment was to his father! Needless to say, my client was overjoyed.

I advised him that he should now form a mutually co-operative relationship with the Irish family, pointing out that they were in a position to give the child the best educational advantages. The sad thing about these cases is that you never get to hear what happened in the end. That little boy will be almost thirty now. I would so love to hear how his life has gone.

In those days junior barristers all started with enormous blue bags made out of something like hard-wearing curtain material, with a huge tasselled rope which you could swing over your shoulder, especially for the purpose of carrying robes, wigs and papers to court. Your initials would be embroidered on them.

Eventually, you graduated to a red bag; the custom was that you were presented with that by someone who had led you in a successful case. Nowadays I suppose the bags have been replaced by those little suitcases on wheels. But Judith gave me my red bag and I still treasure it.

- CHAPTER TWENTY-THREE - SOME GOODBYES - OR *AU REVOIRS*?

John celebrated his eightieth birthday in 2000. We planned a massive celebration, taking all the children and grandchildren to La Manga Club, booking various apartments for the different families. We were there for two weeks, getting together every day for meals, coffees, wines, swimming, occasional golf or tennis and some forays into the surrounding countryside.

On the eve of the big day I stayed to babysit the younger children while the adults and more senior children went to a local piano bar to have a singsong. *Danny Boy,* John's lifelong favourite, top of the list. On the day itself we had a magnificent dinner in the hotel on site, complete with an enormous birthday cake and a good deal of champagne. John loved it all. He was, and is still, adored by his grandchildren.

Mary Rose had brought James with her. We all liked him immensely and hoped that they would marry. But, as mentioned previously, John warned me solemnly. 'James will never marry Mary. He is a typical Irish bachelor.' Exactly what Daddy always used to tell me about John!

They did marry but, sadly, the wedding was not to be until two years later and John was never to see it. At the time though he seemed in perfect health, getting every minute's worth of value from having our family constantly around us.

Maureen and Bill had come from Australia, of course, with their daughters Fiona and Alex.

One day she said to me, 'Mummy, I think you ought to know. I was talking to Daddy and said something about "when Mummy retires". Daddy said, "Your mother retiring is only a pipe dream".'

That was quite a shock. John had insisted on my carrying on at the Bar when he had first retired, ten years earlier. I had no idea that he had changed his mind about it. He would certainly never have told me himself.

I had no trouble deciding what to do. I loved my job, but John and the family had always come first. I had discovered that my fellow tenants in chambers had a nickname for me: 'Mega-Mum'. It was not just the seven children, it was that people tended to come to me if they were worried or upset about something.

One of my colleagues, quite a tough lady, was devastated when her mother died. Shortly afterwards she came into my room when I was alone, closed the door behind her and asked me, 'Do you believe I will see my mother again?'

'I'm sure you will.'

'Well, I can't believe it, but I just wanted to hear you say it.'

John's birthday was in August. When I got back in September I told the head of chambers and my chief clerk that I would be retiring after Christmas; some of my cases had to be finished. They were sad but they understood. In February chambers honoured us with a farewell dinner in Middle Temple, something usually done only if a member became a QC or was appointed to the bench. John was so proud that night.

Our plan was that we would be spending a lot more time in our lovely apartment in La Manga Club, playing golf and hoping to improve our not very impressive handicaps. We arrived in Spain in mid-March. Shortly afterwards, Alice, Pat and their two boys, John and James, came for a week's holiday and we were hoping to see more members of the family in the coming months.

Saying goodbye to them was terribly sad, which was a bit ridiculous as we knew we would be meeting up again soon. For some unknown reason it felt as though this parting was significant. Alice told me afterwards that she cried all the way to the airport. John and I were very sad too when they left.

It was only a few days later that we lost John. He had been in great form the day before, trying to teach me to play bowls – a game in which a friend had given him his first lesson only a week previously. Needless to say, I was hopeless; he wasn't a great teacher and reduced the pair of us to helpless giggles. It was Saturday and we went to the vigil Mass in our local village and enjoyed a meal in his favourite pub. Driving back to our apartment, he promised to take me to my favourite place for lunch the next day.

He was taken ill during the night, but made light of it. I realise now that he knew that it was serious. But all our lives he had been telling me, 'When my time comes, I want to drop dead on the golf course – and if it happens you're not to be upset.'

As a doctor he had been dealing with death all his life and knew the best one to choose. He dreaded hospitalisation. When I had undergone minor surgery a couple of years before, his anxiety about the anaesthetic had resulted in him becoming really ill.

I woke in the middle of that night and he wasn't beside me. I found him hunched up in an armchair. He said he had a bit of tummy upset and came back to bed.

The following day he slept late, got up and dressed, but decided he was tired and went back to have a sleep. I left him in peace for an hour and went in to offer a cup of tea. I thought he had fainted but I was wrong. It was absolutely typical of John that he wanted to spare me the suffering of seeing him die, but it made the shock and grief even worse.

Next morning, the first plane into Alicante from Gatwick brought my sons, Tom and Hugh, my sister Oonagh and her husband John, my daughter Katie and Hugh's wife Karen.

A kind friend drove me to the airport to meet them.

Then followed a nightmare four days, making arrangements to bring him back to England. The officials at the club could not have been more kind, but our insurance company were anything but, first telling us that his insurance did not cover the return of his body. I told them that it didn't matter. I would pay and we could argue about it afterwards. They then admitted that we were covered, but dragged out the time to make the arrangements.

Tom phoned and asked what the problem was. 'Your mother is insisting on flying on the same plane,' he was told. 'Doesn't she know that he'll be in the hold?' And 'It's our money and we want to do it as cheaply as possible.'

John's funeral was amazing – seven priests on the altar and each of the children and grandchildren had a part to play in the Requiem. His old friend Bishop Charles phoned to say he was coming to be the chief celebrant. The church was so packed that latecomers were standing outside on the street – one couple arrived, saw the crowd and concluded that the ceremony was over. Truly he was a much-loved man. And truly he deserved it.

Ami Feder, my then head of chambers was there, with all the other members who could get away. At the reception afterwards Maureen told me, 'Ami is going round the whole family saying, "Your mother must come back".'

Indeed, he and my other friends all tried to persuade me to go back. I thought about it, but by that time much of my practice was involved with cases of child abuse. I knew that it would be unbearable to return to an empty home after a day of watching the recording of some small victim trying to explain what had happened and sobbing so much that what they were trying to say was unintelligible. Often judges, legal representatives and social workers spend whole days viewing the same video over and over again. John's comforting arms around me and the glass of wine he would pour at the end of such days were the only things which could make that endurable for me.

So I decided to become a family mediator. Mediation was in its infancy then. The Bromley centre was the second to be set up in the United Kingdom and dear Fred, who had started it all there, was still in charge. When I contacted him he was, to say the least, unenthusiastic. 'I find that barristers do not make good mediators; they are too used to taking sides,' he told me.

But he was very proud of his set-up and kindly invited me to attend the AGM as a guest. Luckily for me, the chair happened to be a family judge before whom I had made many appearances. He advised Fred to take me on, as he knew I always tried to settle family disputes rather than take them to court.

Mediation does not set out to save the marriage – if there is any hope for that there are organisations specifically designed to help. Mediators are trained to help warring couples to agree matters concerning children or finances without having to go through the court process, saving them money and, hopefully, leaving them with a reasonable relationship, particularly if they have children.

Interestingly, I soon discovered that qualifying as a mediator involved more study than I remembered having to do for my law degree or call to the Bar. I was decades older, of course, and I didn't have John to support me as he always had. His loss was still new and raw.

A few months after he died I had done a course on creative writing at Norwich University. One of the early exercises required us to write the first thing that came into our heads. I filled a whole sheet of foolscap with the word 'lonely' written over and over again. I didn't hand it in.

What kept me going was the unbounded love our children and grandchildren gave me. Without them, I would really have preferred to die myself.

Not only did the mediation course involve a lot of study. We had to spent five weekends in Swindon, with lectures and exercises important for our training. There were about a dozen of us in the group. I drove up the night before the first session, having booked into one of the lodging houses recommended. What about a meal?

I had never before eaten a meal alone in a restaurant. I found a little Italian place, the owner showed me a table and asked if anyone were joining me. I shook my head. He could not have been kinder or more attentive, maybe it was obvious that I had recently been widowed.

When I met my fellow students the following morning things improved. We ate in small groups, even went to the cinema one night. By the time the weekend was over we were friends. I qualified as a mediator and returned to Fred, spending three or four years working at the Bromley centre.

But I soon discovered that I was unable to do financial mediation. As a mediator your task is to help the couple reach outcomes acceptable to both, you cannot cross-examine someone if you believe they are not being completely frank about their finances. In most cases, certainly the ones that came my way, the wife would be in a weaker position than the husband. Many wives in those days had no idea what their husband's income was. It may be different now, I do hope so.

All too often wives would accept financial offers of settlement which worried me. But if they had an agreement, I was not permitted to conduct the kind of investigation which I was used to in a court setting. The very most I was allowed to do was to urge that the wife concerned consult her own solicitor before she signed anything, but not all solicitors are experts in family law. In the end I told Fred that I would prefer to stick to disputes about children.

We had a success rate of over 80% in our children cases, meaning that the parents had agreed arrangements about residence and visiting rights between themselves rather than having recourse to the court room.

We had a defined process to follow. Fred used to say he should be able to come into a room and immediately know what point had been reached. Briefly, I would explain to the couple that each of them would have time alone with me to say what they wanted from the process. They had to choose who went first. When that had been done the couple would return to the room, to find tea and coffee available, together with a box of Kleenex.

I would then repeat what each had said, leaving out anything which they had asked me to keep confidential, requesting no interruptions.

Very often, they would be surprised to find, contrary to their expectations, that perhaps the other parent was not being as intransigent as they had thought, but they would still be looking away from one another. Then came the time when they could ask questions through me. Gradually as that happened they would start to talk between themselves, often having had no contact for weeks or months.

When I asked what the child in dispute would want, I would emphasise that he/she would only wish that their parents could agree about what should happen.

Usually, the whole process would take two or three meetings, but sometimes matters could be agreed on the first appointment. The most satisfactory outcome would be if I heard the parents arranging to meet later for a cup of coffee and further discussion. That was always a magic moment, and it happened more often than you might think.

Jimmy was the first of my siblings to leave us. Growing up together we had been very close. He was a charmer – good looking, great sense of humour, loved a party. We could both play the piano and enjoyed singing duets from the popular musicals of the time. He qualified as a dentist at Guy's hospital where he met Biddy, his beautiful wife. When he and Biddy did the Charleston together other dancers would stop to watch them.

Tragically, while their four children were still young, Jimmy became an alcoholic. Why this happens nobody knows. It is an illness but one with devastating consequences, not only for the sufferer but inevitably for all those who love him too. Obviously it affected Biddy and the children far more than any of us. Eventually there was a divorce; she had no choice.

My mother was distraught. 'What do we do?' she asked.

'We just concentrate on letting those children know

that they still have a Granny, aunties and uncles,' I advised and we all did just that.

Their daughter and three sons are a real credit to Biddy, who brought them up single-handedly, all with good jobs and happy marriages, thank God. Jimmy died in his early sixties. Poor Biddy died very young, but not before she had seen all the children married and settled and welcomed her beloved grandchildren.

- CHAPTER TWENTY-FOUR - MORE ENDINGS AND A NEW BEGINNING

Oonagh's husband John Keefe was diagnosed with cancer. I would drive through the Dartford tunnel to visit them in Brightlingsea where they had chosen to live in their retirement.

We went for a trip through the Constable countryside, as we often did. John stopped the car close to a little wood. 'This is where we are going to be buried,' he told me casually. We walked over to the trees and I could see that some of them had plaques naming those already interred there. Oonagh and he had already chosen the trees they preferred to be planted and booked a site for the planting. 'The grandchildren will be able to visit us and bring picnics,' Oonagh explained.

He and Oonagh never had any fear of death. Their faith and trust in God was absolute. Towards the end of his life John would tell his grandchildren that he was dying and that this was what death was like: in John's case reading to his heart's content, often books about theology or the history of the Catholic church; if he came across a new word he would ask one of the children to look it up for him in his Oxford dictionary.

He enjoyed entertaining his friends to the last – one called a few days before he died to ask if it would be all right if he paid a visit. 'Please do,' was the response, 'but don't bring any unripe bananas!'

Very sadly, Oonagh too was diagnosed with cancer during his illness. I took her to one of her appointments. On our return she gave him a hug and said, 'All well. Now we can concentrate on you!'

All, in fact, was far from being well. Not many months after she lost him, she too was dying. I was heartbroken. Whenever I could I drove over to see her. On one occasion it happened to be Ash Wednesday, a day of fasting in the Church. 'Did you have pancakes yesterday (Shrove Tuesday)?' she enquired.

I replied that I never bothered when I was on my own. 'Well,' she said, 'We'll have some today.'

'Oonagh,' I protested, it's Ash Wednesday!'

'God won't mind,' she assured me.

And He didn't.

Only a few weeks after that I was summoned. She had never admitted any pain, only a 'little discomfort'. But even to my non-medical eyes she had been growing weaker physically, although she maintained the feisty spirit she had always had, walking her beloved terrier Pickwick, tending her garden, chatting to her many friends, never unwilling to utter a strong opinion or a kind word.

Her daughter Dorothy was over from Australia, where she lives. When she arrived she gave me a very upbeat telephone call. She was on her way to Europe to give an address at an international conference on the treatment of cancer, a subject on which she was already an internationally acclaimed expert. She assured me that she found her mother well and in good spirits, taking into account the stage at which her illness was.

But before Dorothy could leave for Europe she called me again. 'I think you would want to be here,' was all she said, and I knew what it meant.

When I got there Oonagh had moved to the same room downstairs where they had made a bed for John's last days. Her seven children had gathered, together with her grandchildren. Our brother Mike, my son Tom and a couple of my other children arrived later.

'Well,' she said, 'We're all here – let's open some champagne!'

A priest who was a devoted friend came and celebrated Mass with us all kneeling round her bed; Pickwick lay beside her on the coverlet. She and John had always called one another 'My dearest dear', half jokingly after the well-known song. They were the last three words I heard her speak. I believe he came back for her. I felt very alone after that, although I still had my dear brother Mike and we spoke on the phone every day. In addition, I had my Yorkshire terrier Toffee, who ruled me with an iron paw.

Michael had posed a problem for my parents when he left school. Sadly, my father had always been over-protective because his youngest child had been born with a spinal deformity. He would never accept that Mike was a highly intelligent as Oonagh and I believed him to be. With us older siblings Daddy had always insisted that we obtain 'a meal ticket', some qualification which would entitle us to earn a living.

But his attitude to Mike was completely different.

When he was about fourteen, and doing absolutely nothing at school because nothing was expected of him, I managed to persuade Daddy to have him assessed at the Tavistock Institute. The report produced stated clearly that Mike was intelligent enough to follow any career he chose, but 'intellectually lazy'.

Daddy's response was tragic: 'They've known him for three days. I've known him all his life.'

Mike left school when he was sixteen. What was he to become? My mother as usual had the answer. She had never used her MA degree, but put it to good use now. She had for several years been interested in antique silver; she offered to work for a year without payment for a local friend who owned an antique shop if, in return, he would teach her all he knew about silver hall marks.

Mummy was over sixty when her year was completed. She took on a half-share in a stall in Gray's Antique Market near Bond Street for a couple of days a week. She continued to learn from all the collectors with whom she came into contact and at the same time she trained Mike in the antique silver business, with particular regard to rare Irish hall marks.

Within a few short years she and Mike were in partnership and had a shop in St Christopher's Place, just behind Selfridges, selling silver and antique jewellery, which Mummy introduced as a sideline to their business. Mike began writing articles about Irish silver for specialist magazines; he became a member of the Goldsmiths' Company.

The 'bible' for antique silver enthusiasts is a huge

volume entitled *Jackson's Silver and Gold Marks of England Scotland and Ireland,* first published as *English Goldsmiths and their Marks* in 1905. It was 1989 when the title was changed to embrace Scotland and Ireland. Mike was invited to edit the Irish section – a labour of love as far as he was concerned. From that time on he was the go-to man for Irish Museum experts doubtful about obscure silver marks. So Mummy had created a career for him which he thoroughly enjoyed for the remainder of his life.

Never married, he cared for my mother until we lost her at the age of ninety. Daddy had died some years earlier at the age of seventy-six. After Mummy's death, Mike devoted himself to looking after our brother Jimmy, at times a thankless and difficult task in view of Jimmy's addiction. He was adored by all his many nephews and nieces, not least for his wry sense of humour. 'When I can't sleep,' he used to tell them. 'I don't count sheep, I count my father's descendants.'

His own health gradually deteriorated. Bent over by his deformity, he struggled to walk, obviously in pain but never admitting it. At one point I accompanied him to a hospital appointment at St Mary's, Paddington to see a cardiologist. He was advised that he needed surgery. He turned it down.

In the meantime, Neil Clarke lost his beloved wife Sonia. We had been good friends for so many years after meeting on our first day at King's. Sonia and he were so kind to me after I lost John, always including me in dinner parties, playing bridge, hearing opera at Covent Garden, even going on a couple of cruises together.

They were amazing ballroom dancers, having taught themselves to televised lessons by Victor Sylvester. I always retired to my cabin after dinner because poor Neil would have felt that he ought to ask me to dance and I was never in Sonia's league.

Sonia and I were close friends, on the board of the Catholic Truth Society, and on the Catholic Union committee, which met monthly at the House of Lords to consider and advise on the response of the Church to any projected legislation on which it was felt that we should have a voice. Sonia was a distinguished historian and became the chief history examiner for the International Baccalaureate.

Neil had trained as an accountant after obtaining his LL.B. In 1969 he joined the industrial and engineering group Charter Consolidated, ending up as chief executive and deputy chairman. In 1991 he was appointed chairman of British Coal, his task being to oversee the privatisation of an industry in decline. He successfully battled the government to get decent compensation for the miners who lost their jobs.

His popularity with the miners was manifest when six of their leaders attended his funeral to tell me how much they appreciated what he had done for them.

He lost Sonia in exactly the same way that I had lost John ten years previously – she died suddenly, abroad. He was inconsolable. I have never seen a man weep so much. At least I could tell him that I knew exactly how he was feeling.

He invited me out to dinner a couple of times, and we reminisced about John and Sonia. Two months after Sonia died, however, I was diagnosed with breast cancer. Coward that I am, I told the surgeon that I did not want any surgery or radiation treatment, I'd had a good life and I just wanted to be kept out of pain until the end.

Needless to say, this was not a popular decision with my children. But I thought it was the right one for me, until Neil sat me down with a glass of wine one day and told me that I couldn't do this to my family. He said, 'I promise I will see you through whatever it means, but if you might have a few more years it's unfair not to go ahead with what the consultant advises.'

That he did, and by the time I had been through it all we were becoming very close. So eventually we decided to get married. Turning up at the register office at the age of eighty, accompanied by my 'toy boy' prospective husband of seventy-six, did not deter the official from putting us separately through a rigorous questionnaire designed to ensure that one of us was not seeking marriage in order to gain British citizenship or for some other nefarious purpose which I can't imagine.

But we did manage to persuade her of our good intentions, even though Neil couldn't remember the date of my birthday. A few weeks later dear Father Tom married us in my parish church in the presence of our ten children and eighteen grandchildren. Neil decided that on top of those numbers we were only allowed to invite two friends each. Mike was there of course, although too ill to climb the altar steps for the group photograph, something I still regret.

What we did not know was that Neil was already

suffering from advanced cancer himself. The wedding was in March. By August he was in such pain that he agreed to see a consultant. Tragically, it was too late; the cancer had spread everywhere.

The following months would have been unendurable had it not been for the loving support of our families and friends. The chemotherapy was exhausting and completely useless. The medics simply never got his pain under control. He bore it all with such patience and dignity. At last I was realising why John had always prayed for the sudden death he was granted.

Neil had a bad fall in the house and had to be admitted to hospital, despite his determined resistance. We were asked what our care plan was. I told them that I was caring for him.

They shook their heads and wouldn't release him until we had arranged professional nursing care twenty-four hours a day.

Without exception, his carers adored him, appreciating his unwavering courtesy and gratitude. When things were at their worst, Father Tom visited regularly, despite the the fact that we were not his parishioners. He would give Neil his large crucifix to hold while he was giving us the Eucharist. The day came when Neil refused to release his grip to return the cross. 'It's doing more good here than in my bag,' Father Tom told me.

Father Tom was with Neil the night before he died. Neil died holding his cross. We had been married eight months.

But I am a firm believer that Almighty God always

has a plan. The only thing Neil really wanted was to die in his own home. Any of his sons would have had him in their homes when he became so ill. That is not what would have made him happy. I was able to see to it that he spent his last days in his living room, downstairs, where he could look out at the garden he loved so much and listen to his favourite operatic arias.

Again, the pain of his loss was terrible. But that was not to be the end of grief. A few weeks later Mike too went to his eternal reward. He was only sixty-one years old.

There is a downside to reaching your nineties, so many losses to cope with – old friends as well as family members. You might think you'd get used to it. You don't.

But with a clan as big as ours there is always something to look forward to: my first great grandchild, Arlo William, arrived on 2nd November 2020 – my twenty-first descendant! Another adorable baby in the family after seventeen years!

My Catholic faith, shared with John and Neil, has helped me get through the lonely times, as has my wonderful family. I firmly believe that everything that happens has a purpose – we may not know it at the time, but looking back you can see a pattern. And I believe that the day will come when we will meet all our loved ones again in a place where there will never be any more goodbyes.

As my loving friend Canon Joe said to me once, 'Even if we're all wrong, dear, we've had happier lives believing it.'

How very true.

- CHAPTER TWENTY-FIVE -
UP TO NOW

Widowed for a second time, I returned to my home in Bickley. Toffee had taken an instant dislike to Neil and adamantly refused to behave herself when kindly invited to stay with him, making her feelings plain by leaving little puddles on his precious carpets – something which she would never have dreamt of doing at home.

In the end I honestly had to choose between her and Neil. Luckily, she had not one but two alternative homes where she was loved and fussed over whenever I had been going away on holiday. My friend Audrey had been dog-sitting for Toffee since I had first acquired her. Michael and Maria, with their daughter Carmela, were also devoted to her. So there had been no problem in finding her a new home where she would be happy.

Now she could come back to me, which helped a little with my sadness.

My family too were a welcome distraction. The grandchildren were growing up, most of them at school. We were all together on one occasion, when James cornered me and, to my surprise and delight, asked for my consent to his marriage to Mary Rose. All I could think of was how pleased John would have been to be proved wrong, as Daddy had been about him.

The wedding was to be in Cornwall where James's family lived. He and Mary Rose took me down to meet his parents, Brian and Mary. They were originally from Northern Ireland and we were friends from the start.

To tell the truth, I was dreading making the wedding arrangements without John. But the Gelstons were a marvellous support, introducing me to the pretty little church where their other son William had been married, finding a fabulous venue in the grounds of a stately home, helping to deal with caterers and flowers.

I went to my favourite dress shop with Alice and tried to find a new outfit to wear. John had always taken such an interest in my clothes. He would come with me to try things on, sitting outside the changing room, often supplied with a cup of coffee by the salesgirls. I would emerge dressed in the new outfit and he would pronounce his judgment. Not typical of your average Irishman, but John would go so far as to ask me to try something which he had spotted in a shop window and thought would suit me.

So when Alice had selected a few items for me to try I just burst into tears. I missed him so much. My great friend Eileen MacCann was having none of this. 'I'm taking you up to the fashion designers sale in Chelsea Town Hall,' she announced, determined not to take 'no' for an answer. Once there, she began frisking the racks with her incredible eye, coming back with armfuls of gorgeous outfits and insisting that I tried them all on.

When she had decided on her choice she wanted to

know about a hat. I assured her that I had a perfectly good one in my wardrobe, which I had purchased a few years ago in Marks and Spencer. She was horrified. 'You are not wearing any hat from Marks and Spencer to your daughter's wedding,' she told me flatly.

Eileen herself, an enthusiastic race-goer, has so many beautiful hats that she has to keep them in boxes adorned with photographs of their contents so that she can find them easily. She was my GP after John died and very quickly and kindly took me under her wing, inviting me round for family meals and to events at the golf club. Her dear husband John was my bank manager, as it happens; the pair of them never willingly missed Ascot, Cheltenham, Epsom or any of the important Irish meetings.

I have to confess that I know nothing about racing, but they did bring me to Ascot for one unforgettable day. We set off in a chauffeur driven car with the boot crammed with smoked salmon, cold meats, salads and champagne. While we progressed to the royal enclosure the driver laid up the picnic in the car park. Eileen had, of course, provided me with a suitable hat.

Eileen's hats had all been selected from the top milliners in London. The one she lent me was adorned with ostrich feathers and its colour was a perfect match for the outfit for Mary Rose's wedding which she had chosen. I have borrowed it twice since, once for the Ascot outing and again more recently for my grandson's wedding.

At Ascot we met so many of John and Eileen's friends, visited a marvellously sited box looking over the finishing line for more champagne and finished up, once the races were over, at a party where most of the guests seemed to be owners or jockeys. I know nothing about horses but I could see what a great time everyone was having.

The MacCanns have a beautiful apartment in Las Palmas in the Canaries, where they spend a good deal of time now that both have retired. They have invited me many times to share the most wonderful holidays there. I always booked a room, overlooking the incredibly long stretch of perfect beach, in the Reina Isabel, a fantastic hotel a few minutes' walk away from their home, and pottered about during the day, attending Mass, walking and shopping. Every evening we would meet up for a barbecue on their roof terrace or a meal in one of the many restaurants in the resort, shared with their friends.

They knew me well in the hotel. Many of the MacCanns' friends in Las Palmas are gay, which meant that I would be escorted back there every night by a different man. Eyebrows might have been raised at first but the reception staff got used to that.

Alice's husband Pat is Greek Cypriot; he owns some property in Larnaca including a beautiful apartment, his family home, overlooking St Lazarus basilica. I have shared some lovely holidays with them, sometimes with Nora and Katie. I have been on a few cruises too, since being widowed, some with Jofan Bankes, after we met playing bridge at the Reform Club, and some with another dear friend, Maureen Kiely.

I managed to get over to Australia to visit Maureen and her family on a couple of occasions:

Mary Rose, James, Nora and I took Rosie when she was only a few months old. Travelling with a gorgeous baby, I discovered, entitled us to top star treatment in airports and planes. On another occasion Matthew, Jimmy's youngest, was having a marvellous beach wedding and Nora and I went over for that.

Now that I am in my nineties I fear that my travelling days may be done, but you never know…

Toffee and I were both feeling our years when I began to look around for somewhere more convenient to live. My home was a two-storey four-bedroom detached house in a quiet little close of twelve similar properties. We were all friendly with one another, but I became particularly fond of Norma and Maurice who lived opposite.

They owned a care home nearby and insisted that if I ever needed help, even during the night, they would be there for me, pointing out that they were used to night calls in their business. Unfortunately, I had to take them up on the offer one night when Toffee had decided that she definitely needed to go out in the garden right that minute.

Half dazed with sleep, I picked her up and started downstairs. Somehow my foot slipped on the carpet and I ended up smacking my head into the wall facing the end of the staircase.

At four in the morning, streaming with blood, I called their number. They came over immediately and drove me to the local hospital, still bleeding heavily, in Maurice's precious car, the pride of his life, without one word about what was undoubtedly happening to its upholstery. Both nurses kept asking me about whether

I had any pain in my neck which puzzled me, as they could see that the wound was on the top of my head. Thankfully, it was only when we talked about it afterwards that I realised they had been concerned about whether I had broken my neck.

They stayed with me at the hospital while I was given six stitches in the wound. I was able to phone Alice at about eight in the morning, and they stayed until she arrived to collect me.

It was after this accident that I began to consider whether I ought to move. John and I had always loved London and I wondered if there might be some sort of retirement place I could find there.

It was Norma who told me about my present home, at that time under construction. Kathleen had already discovered it because she was considering moving from her large property not too far away from the building site. Norma had found an advertisement in one of the Sunday papers and showed it to me. They were thinking about it, but when Maurice telephoned to confirm that there would be parking for his car and was told there wouldn't he lost interest.

Maureen happened to be over on a visit from Australia at the time; she, Alice and I decided to go and have a look. The place was still very much under construction but they had a show flat and a model of what it would be like. It was to be a community of people aged over sixty-five, offering leasehold apartments for sale. There would be one hundred and three residences in two blocks with a garden in between. It faced one of the London parks and would have a restaurant. Added to this, all the apartments had their own kitchens, in addition to a communal gym, cinema and swimming pool. To compensate for the lack of parking there would be drivers on duty to take us shopping and on individual trips.

An important aspect for me at the time was that buyers who owned dogs would be allowed to bring them, as long as they were not inconveniencing other residents. Sadly, poor Toffee had departed this world before the time came to live there.

I fell in love with the whole concept that very day, and put down a deposit of £5,000 on the promise that, if I changed my mind for any reason before the date when the full deposit would be due, it would be completely refundable.

It was not until about two years later that I was able to move into my new home. The building was completed in April 2016 but, like many others at the time, I had a great deal of trouble selling my own property and needed to raise that money to complete my purchase.

I moved in at the beginning of October 2016 and have never regretted it for a second. Many of the other residents have become dear friends, and the staff are all more kind and caring than any of us have a right to expect, cherished friends as well. Those four years have passed so quickly and happily!

One of the greatest advantages of living here is that my grandchildren, the majority based in London, are able to visit me whenever they have a chance. In Bickley I would never have been so involved in their lives. Having Nora living in London too has given us both the benefit of shared leisure activities and constant contact with one another.

As I write, however, we are in the grip of coronavirus. Life for all of us has changed dramatically. Sometimes it seems that things have always been like this: living our separate lives, wearing gloves and face masks when we leave our apartments, having contact with family members only over the phone or on the Internet, endlessly washing our hands in hot soapy water, having food and other necessities delivered to our apartments, not having cushions on the garden chairs, being alone most of the time. The restaurant is open but you have to sit alone at a table, the cinema has films but only a few people can be accommodated, the minibus still takes those who are prepared to go shopping, but only four people are allowed to travel in it. If you want to go for a swim or into the gym you have to book an appointment; if you have no live-in partner you must go alone.

For the anniversary of D-Day, something which the majority here actually lived through, a neighbour phoned and suggested that the occupants of the four apartments on my floor should simply open their doors, bring chairs outside them and have individual cups of tea to celebrate, but that was deemed to be too risky. However, we do accept that the decisions made are to protect us.

My eldest son Hugh fell ill in early March. I hadn't heard from him for several days, which was unusual; one of my daughters explained that he hadn't been feeling well but was on the mend. He phoned me later that day, sounding very tired, to tell me that he thought he had been suffering from the COVID-19 virus but believed that he had recovered.

I now know he was being slightly economical with the truth for my benefit, as sons tend to be; the next thing I heard was that he had been admitted to his local hospital in Bath. It was only later I learned that his wife Karen, desperately concerned about him, had been dialling 111 and his GP for days before his admission.

On Mothering Sunday he managed to call me on his mobile from the intensive care unit, but his voice was so weak that I could hardly understand what he was saying. The following day came an even more distressing call. He wanted to tell me himself that he was being put into an induced coma so that they could place him in a ventilator. He was sixty-five. I now know that he believed that might be the last time he would ever speak to me.

He spent nine days in the ventilator. The disease attacked not only his lungs but his heart and kidneys as well.

All the family and all our friends were praying for him. One very loving and supportive friend told me he didn't believe in God but would say his own kind of prayers – they worked, so I told him that God obviously believed in him! But Hugh really had a tsunami of prayer and I believed that somehow he would be conscious of that and it would give him strength.

It took the hospital three days to revive him from the coma. As soon as he was able, he called me, with the assistance of a nurse, still sounding weak and exhausted. I admit shedding a few tears hearing his voice again; then I apologised because my mobile had locked itself for some reason and we couldn't see one another on FaceTime.

He laughed and said, 'Mum, every time we meet up you have something wrong with some bit of technology.' That laugh was the most wonderful sound I could have heard.

When he left the intensive care unit for an ordinary ward in a wheelchair, all the doctors and nursing staff there lined up to applaud him.

Later, when we were all coming out of our homes on Thursday nights to cheer for the NHS, Hugh was the one making the most noise. God has been very good to us all.

Thankfully, we were given some respite from the pandemic over the summer months. I celebrated my ninetieth birthday in July with twenty-eight of my immediate family. Poor Maureen and Bill could not come from Australia as they had planned to do, again because of the virus.

But we were able to celebrate over in the park, with individual picnics prepared by our excellent chef here, Kristian, and a good deal of champagne, with a gorgeous surprise birthday cake to follow. My son-in-law's trumpet enabled us to keep well socially distanced from other people in the park and we observed social distancing between ourselves.

John used to like the motto: 'This also will pass,' using it in good times and in bad. He also used to say, 'It's the bad times that make the good times.'

How blessed have I been to have so many of those good times.

About the Author

Born in Glasgow in 1930 to parents with an Irish background, Maureen spent the first seven years of her life with her maternal grandmother and younger sister Oonagh. Her father and mother were in Nigeria where her father was a doctor.

Enrolled at a convent boarding school at the age of eleven, Maureen had attended four different schools in two different educational systems. Plump, clumsy, overweight and easily made to cry, she was the object of mild bullying for several years. Her tormentors were all going to university so she resolved never to follow them there.

Three years later she changed her mind and decided she would like to study law. On the day she was awarded a place at King's College, London, she met her first husband, John Mullally, a doctor like her father. They married in her first summer vacation; their happy marriage lasted for forty-seven years. Despite the birth of their first child Hugh during her studies, she obtained her LL.B with her fellow students. Two years later she was called to the Bar.

Hugh was followed by six siblings all born within ten years. At home with the children Maureen was contributing articles to women's magazines and talks to BBC Woman's Hour.

When Hugh was nearly eighteen Maureen started her pupillages in Middle Temple, practising family law for twenty-seven years until John's sudden death in 2000.

Having met at King's, Neil Clarke and his wife Sonia had become their lifelong friends. The last chairman of British Coal, Neil was responsible for insisting the government pay good compensation to the miners on the pit closures.

In 2011, both widowed, Maureen and Neil married. Sadly the marriage only lasted eight months, Shortly after it took place, Neil was diagnosed with cancer.